Nita Mehta's™

UN-FRIED & BAKED SNACKS

Vegetarian

Enjoy snacks without Deep frying!

Nita Mehta

B.Sc. (Home Science), M.Sc. (Food and Nutrition)
Gold Medalist

SNAB
Excellence in Books

Nita Mehta's™

UN-FRIED & BAKED SNACKS

Vegetarian

Enjoy snacks without Deep frying!

SNAB Excellence in Books
Snab Publishers Pvt Ltd

Corporate Office
3A/3, Asaf Ali Road, New Delhi 110 002
Phone: +91 11 2325 2948, 2325 0091
Telefax: +91 11 2325 0091
E-mail: nitamehta@nitamehta.com
Website: www.nitamehta.com

Editorial and Marketing office
E-159, Greater Kailash II, New Delhi 110 048

Food Styling and Photography by Snab
Typesetting by National Information Technology Academy
3A/3, Asaf Ali Road, New Delhi 110 002

Recipe Development & Testing:
Nita Mehta Foods - R & D Centre
3A/3, Asaf Ali Road, New Delhi - 110002

NITA MEHTA FOODS

ISBN 978-81-7869-380-4

First Edition 2013

Cover Designed by: SNAB Excellence in Books

Printed in India at Infinity Advertising Services (P) Ltd, New Delhi

Distributed by :
NITA MEHTA BOOKS
3A/3, Asaf Ali Road, New Delhi - 02
Distribution Centre :
D16/1, Okhla Industrial Area, Phase-I,
New Delhi - 110020
Tel.: 26813199, 26813200
E-mail: nitamehta.mehta@gmail.com

Nita Mehta Books
Distributors & Publishers

Contributing Writers :
Anurag Mehta
Tanya Mehta
Subhash Mehta
Editors :
Sangeeta
Sunita

Price: Rs. 295/-

Introduction

No more boring fruits or salads or boiled veggies when you feel like eating something light with less calories! This book has delicious Non-fried Snacks which will satisfy your cravings as well as keep your weight in check. The snacks are delicious and nourishing besides being low in calories. A few are pan fried but they use a very little quantity of oil to do so.

The section on "party snacks in minutes" is so good that you will never feel lazy to cook these recipes in just a few minutes to entertain unexpected guests. With the world getting calorie conscious day-by-day, these recipes will be perfect for your parties as well. Baked samosas and kachouris will be a treat without feeling guilty. Tikkas and kebabs are all made the low fat way!

There is a section on delicious Snacky Dinner, made really filling, yet very low in calories. The snacks are all steamed, baked, grilled or very lightly pan cooked.

We believe that this book shall prove very useful for the health conscious people, without hampering with the taste of foods.

Nita Mehta

CONTENTS

SNACKS FROM THE PAN 65

FULL MEAL SNACKS 80

DIPS FOR SNACKS 96

Baked & Steamed Snacks

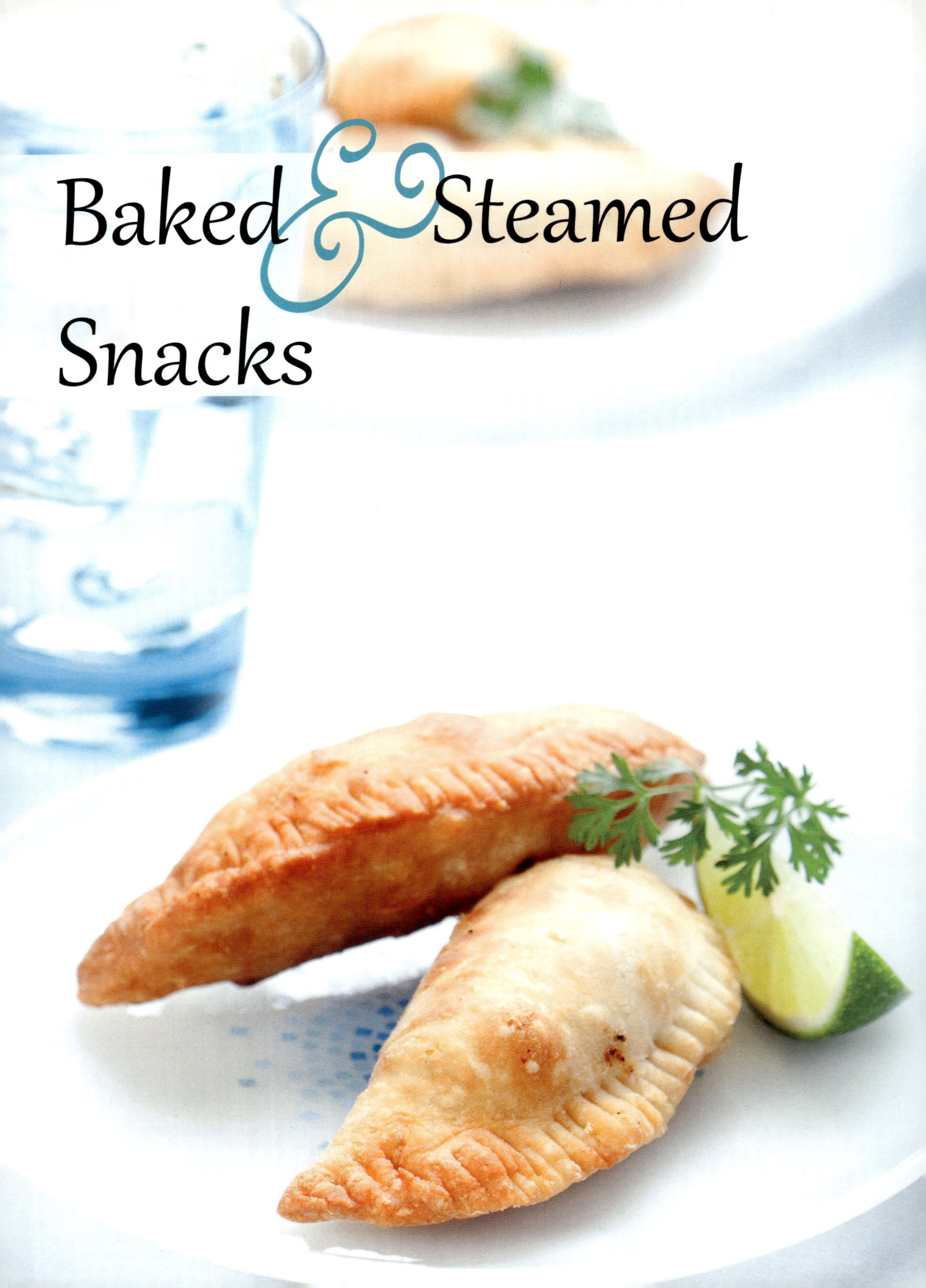

Veggie Squares

Serves 8

2 cups grated cabbage, 1 cup grated carrot, 1½ cups gram flour (*besan*)

1½ cups water, 1 tsp very finely chopped ginger

2 tbsp oil, ½ cup yogurt, 1 tsp lemon juice

½ cup finely grated fresh coconut or dry coconut powder

3 tbsp fresh coriander, ¼ tsp baking soda (*mitha soda*)

1½ tsp cumin (*jeera*) powder, 1¼ tsp red chilli powder

1½-2 tsp salt, or to taste

FOR TOPPING

1 tbsp white sesame seeds (*til*)

1. Except sesame seeds, mix all ingredients together well.
2. Put in a greased medium sized, shallow baking dish to get ½" thick layer (9-10" square or rectangular dish). Sprinkle some sesame seeds (*til*) on top.
3. Bake at 180°C/350°F for 50-60 minutes till it turns brownish. Check with a knife to see if it is done. Leave aside to cool.
4. Cut into 1" squares only after it cools down. To serve, heat on a pan or in a microwave to just make it slightly warm.

Peas Basket

Makes 15

15 bread slices

3 cups boiled peas

1 tbsp finely chopped walnuts

1 tsp chopped ginger

1 radish (*mooli*) - chopped finely

1 tsp chopped green chillies

juice of 1 lemon

salt, pepper and chaat masala to taste

1 carrot, for making the handles

1. Take one slice of bread and roll out thinly with the help of a rolling pin. Cut bread into a round. Apply similar method to all bread slices. Grease muffin tin cups with a little oil. Press each bread round into the muffin tin cup. Bake for 10 minutes at 180°C or till golden brown and crisp.
2. For the filling, boil 3 cups of peas in salted water. Blend 2 cups of boiled peas in the blender till it turns into a coarse paste. In the peas paste mix in finely chopped walnuts, chopped ginger, chopped radish and chopped green chillies. Add whole peas. Squeeze in juice of lemon. Add salt, pepper and chaat masala to taste.
3. To serve, peel carrot and cut lengthwise into ¼" thick slices. Cut each slice into ¼" broad strips, about 6" long. Fill the baked cups with peas. Curve carrot strip over like a handle on the assembled bread cup after you have put in the filling. Serve.

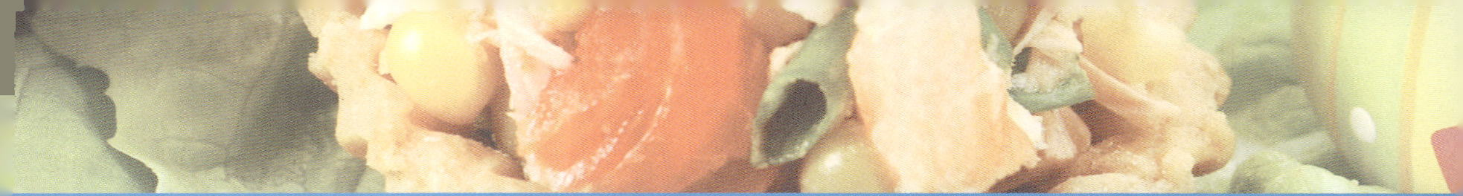

Mexican Corn Tartlets

Makes 16

FOR THE TARTLETS

½ cup maize flour, ¼ cup plain flour (*maida*)

½ tsp salt, 1 tbsp oil, ½ tsp oregano

½ tsp chilli flakes

FOR THE FILLING

2-3 tbsp ready made salsa

1 cup yellow american corn, boiled

1 jalapeno or 1 green chilli - deseeded and chopped

1 tomato - chopped

1 onion - finely chopped

2-3 flakes garlic - chopped

½ cup finely chopped green bell pepper or finely sliced french beans

2 tbsp olive oil

3-4 tbsp grated cheese

½ tsp salt, or to taste

1 tsp paprika, ½ tsp cumin powder *(jeera powder)*

1. For the tartlets, make a soft dough with both flours, salt, oregano, chilli flakes and oil. Divide the dough into 4 parts. Take one part, roll it out into a 7" round and cut 4 smaller rounds out of it, that you will be able to fit into small tart cases. Repeat this with all the 4 rounds.
2. Prick with a fork and lightly bake in a hot oven at 180°C for 10-15 minutes, until crisp. Remove from the oven and let them cool. Store in air-tight container.
3. For the filling, heat oil in a medium frying pan. Add garlic and onion and fry for 2-3 minutes. Add bell peppers/beans and jalapeno. Cook until soft.
4. Add tomatoes and cook for a minute more. Add salsa and stir for a second. Then add the corn, salt, cumin and paprika. Check seasonings. Mix well. Add cheese.
5. Fill the mixture in the tartlets while the mixture is hot and serve immediately garnished with a fresh coriander leaf, with salsa on the side.

Baked Samosa

Makes 8

2 cups plain flour (*maida*)

½ cup warm oil

½ tsp carom seeds (*ajwain*)

¾ tsp salt

½ cup warm water - to knead

FILLING

3 tbsp oil, ½ tsp cumin seeds (*jeera*)

1 tsp coriander seeds (*saboot dhania*) - crushed

1 tbsp ginger-garlic paste

1 green chilli - chopped

½ cup peas - boiled

3 potatoes - boiled and roughly mashed

1 tbsp coriander (*dhania*) powder, 1 tsp cumin (*jeera*) powder

1 tsp garam masala, 1 tsp salt

½ tsp each - dry mango powder (*amchoor*), red chilli powder, turmeric powder (*haldi*)

1. Mix flour, salt, carom seeds and oil together. Add enough warm water to get a soft dough.
2. For filling, heat oil. Add crushed coriander and cumin and stir till golden. Add peas, ginger-garlic, green chilli and turmeric. Stir for 2 minutes. Add potatoes and all the remaining ingredients. Cook for 2-3 minutes. Remove from heat and keep aside.
3. Divide the dough into 4 balls. Roll out each ball to a round *chapatti*. Cut each into half. Pick up one half and bring the straight ends together to make a cone. Overlap the edges together and seal using water. Put filling into the cone. Close it with the help of water.
4. Brush with oil. Bake in a preheated oven at 185°C for 25 minutes on a greased baking tray, turn in between until brown on both sides.

Peshawari Broccoli Tikka

Serves 6

500 gm (2 medium heads) broccoli - cut into medium sized florets with long stalks

2 tsp salt, 1 tsp sugar

1ST MARINADE

juice of 1 lemon (3-4 tsp)

½ tsp carom seeds (*ajwain*)

1 tsp salt and ½ tsp red chilli powder

2ND MARINADE

1 cup thick yogurt - hang for one hour

2 tbsp grated cheese, 2 tbsp oil

4 tbsp cream or fresh malai

2 tbsp roasted cashews - grind with a little water to a paste

1 tbsp cornflour

2 tsp ginger paste, ½ tsp red chilli paste, optional

½ tsp salt, ½ tsp garam masala

1 clove (*laung*) - crushed

seeds of 2 green cardamoms - crushed

1. Boil 5-6 cups of water in a large pan. Add 2 tsp salt and 1 tsp sugar to the water. Add broccoli pieces to the boiling water. Boil. Keep on boiling for a minute. Remove from heat and let broccoli be in hot water for 2 minutes. Drain. Refresh with cold water. Strain. Wipe the pieces well with a clean kitchen towel till well dried.
2. Spread the broccoli on a flat plate and sprinkle the ingredients of the 1st marinade. Marinate the broccoli for 15 minutes.
3. For the 2nd marinade, mix cheese and oil till well blended. Add remaining ingredients and mix well. Pick up the broccoli pieces, leaving the water behind, and add to the yogurt marinade and mix well. Check salt. Refrigerate till the time of serving.
4. To serve, brush the grill rack of the oven or tandoor with some oil. Place the broccoli pieces on it and cook in a preheated oven at 210°C/410°F only for 10 minutes. Do not over cook it, it turns too dry. Serve hot.

Feta Bruschetta with Roasted Peppers

Serves 6-8

1 french loaf

4 tbsp (50 gm) butter

2 flakes garlic - crushed

1 tsp oregano

TOPPING

1 large red capsicum (red bell pepper)

1½ tbsp olive oil

½ cup sliced black olives, optional

200 gm feta cheese or paneer - cut into ¼" cubes

1 large spring onion - finely chopped with greens or 2 tbsp chopped onion

1 tsp oregano, 1 tsp chilli flakes, ¾ tsp salt, or to taste

1 tbsp tomato ketchup

a few basil leaves

PUT LATER

½ cup finely grated parmesan or cheddar cheese

1. Melt butter, add garlic and oregano. Cut french loaf into ½" thick slices. Brush garlic butter on both sides of each slice. Grill on both sides until lightly toasted.
2. To roast the bell pepper, wash and prick the bell pepper with a fork. Rub olive oil all over on it. Hold it directly on a flame till blackened. Alternately, grill in an oven turning occasionally, until blackened on all sides. Cool, peel or rub off the charred skin, deseed and chop into small pieces.
3. Place roasted capsicum in a bowl, add 1 tbsp olive oil and mix well. Add all other ingredients of the topping and toss lightly.
4. Top the toasted slices with the feta/paneer mixture and sprinkle finely grated cheese on top. Serve as it or grill for 2-3 minutes till cheese melts. Serve immediately, garnished with a fresh basil leaf.

Steamed Muthia

A famous Gujrati snack. Steamed rolls of fenugreek or bottle gourd with 3 kinds of flours.

Serves 6

1 cup wheat flour, (*atta*) 1 tbsp semolina (*suji*), 2 tbsp gram flour (*besan*)

1 cup chopped fenugreek leaves (*methi*) or grated bottle gourd (*lauki*)

1 tbsp finely chopped coriander leaves

3 tbsp oil

1 tsp sugar, 1 tsp lemon juice

¼ tsp turmeric powder (*haldi*), ½ tsp red chilli powder, 1 tsp coriander (*dhania*) powder

1½ tsp salt, ¼ tsp baking soda (*mitha soda*)

GRIND TO PASTE

2 green chillies, ½" piece ginger

TEMPERING

2 tsp oil, 1 tsp mustard seeds (*rai*), 1 tsp sesame seeds (*til*)

1. Mix wheat flour, semolina, gram flour in a bowl.
2. Add chopped fenugreek or grated bottle gourd and ginger-green chilli paste. Mix. Add all the other ingredients, except those for tempering. Mix well.
3. Bind the mixture together. Add 1-2 tbsp water if required.
4. Apply some oil to the hands and make a thick, long roll of about 6-8" length from the mixture.
5. Steam the roll. To steam the rolls, boil water in a pan. Place a metal strainer on the pan of boiling water and place the roll in the strainer. Cover with a lid and steam the rolls till done. To steam in a pressure cooker, after the first whistle keep it on slow fire for 7-8 minutes. A tooth pick inserted in the roll should come out clean when the roll is done.
6. Cool and cut the roll into ½" thick slices. Heat a frying pan with oil. Add mustard seeds. As the mustard seeds splutters, add sesame seeds. Stir for a few seconds.
7. Add the muthia slices and saute for a while. Serve.

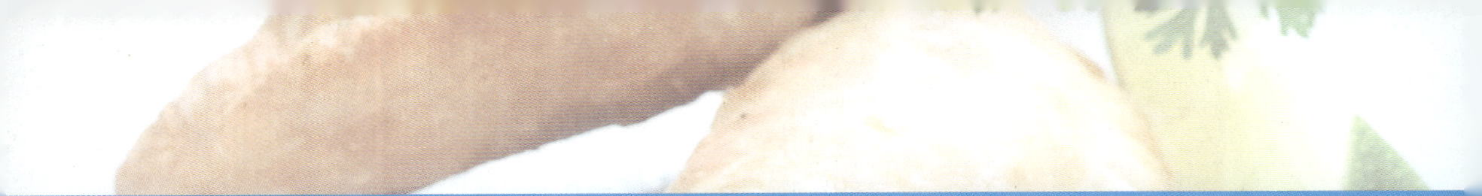

Lebanese Sambousik

Makes 12-15

¼ cup cornflour
¾ cup flour (*maida*)
½ tsp salt, ½ tsp sugar
3 tbsp oil, ¼ cup water

FILLING

150 gms grated paneer (cottage cheese)
¾ cup finely chopped fresh parsley or coriander
2 green chillies - deseeded and finely chopped
1 small onion - finely chopped
½ tsp red chilli powder, ¾ tsp salt, ½ tsp pepper
2 tsp Lebanese spice powder, see page 83

1. Mix all ingredients of the dough. Add enough water to make a firm dough. Knead the dough very well till smooth & elastic. Cover & leave aside for 30 minutes.
2. For the filling, mix all the ingredients of the filling and keep aside.
3. Divide dough into 3 balls. Roll out to a big round. Cut round circles of 2-3" diameter with a cookie cutter.
4. Put filling on one side of a circle. Fold over one end to make a semicircle. Press edges with fingers so that they stick together. Use a little water for sticking. Again cut the edge with a cookie cutter to get a serrated edge. Alternately, press edges with a fork.
5. Brush with olive oil. Bake at 200°C for about 25 minutes till golden brown on both sides. Keep aside till serving time.
6. To serve, grill for 3-4 minutes. Serve hot with tomato ketchup or any dip.

Mushroom Croquettes

Makes 6

2 tbsp butter, 2 tbsp oil
3 tbsp plain flour (*maida*)
2 tbsp semolina (*suji*)
1 tsp crushed garlic
1 tsp finely chopped green chillies
1 cup chopped mushrooms, 1 cup milk
2-3 tbsp corn kernels - crushed
2 tbsp chopped parsley or green coriander
¾ tsp salt, ½ tsp black pepper
½ tsp red chilli flakes, ½ tsp oregano
2 cubes cheddar cheese - grated (4 tbsp)
1 bread slice - churned in a mixer to get fresh crumbs (½ cup)
½ cup crumbled paneer (50 gm)

COATING INGREDIENTS

2 tbsp flour (*maida*), 2 tbsp melted butter or oil
3 slices bread - churned in a mixer to get fresh bread crumbs (1½ cups)

1. Heat oil and butter. Add garlic, green chillies & mushrooms. Saute for 2 minutes.
2. Sprinkle flour and semolina on the mushrooms and saute for a minute.
3. Add 1 cup milk. Stir constantly till very thick and the mixture leaves the sides of the pan. Add corn and mix well for a minute. Remove from fire. Add coriander/parsley, salt, pepper, red chilli flakes, oregano and cheese. Mix well. Let it cool.
4. Add paneer and bread crumbs. Mix lightly. Check seasonings. Shape into rolls. Roll on a flat surface to make uniform croquettes. Press the sides against the surface to get neat sides.
5. For coating, roll a croquette over flour spread on a plate. Dip in ½ cup water. Again roll over bread crumbs mixed with 2 tbsp butter/oil. Refrigerate till serving.
6. Bake on a greased baking tray at 200°C for 20-25 minutes or till golden. If you like, put under a grill for 2-3 minutes. Serve hot.

Spicy Potato Batons

Serves 4

2 large potatoes (or 200 gm paneer may be used)

1 tbsp grated or very finely chopped garlic

1 tbsp lemon juice, 2 tbsp oil, ½-¾ tsp salt

1 tbsp very finely grated cheddar and 1 tbsp very finely grated mozzarella cheese

DRY ROAST TOGETHER

2 dry red chillies - deseeded, 1 tsp coriander seeds (*saboot dhania*)

½ tsp cumin seeds, 4 black pepper corns, 2" piece cinnamon

4 cloves (*laung*), ¼ tsp nutmeg (*jaiphal*) powder

1. Cut potatoes into ¼" thick slices. Cut slices into ¼" broad fingers or batons. Boil potatoes in 4 cups water with 1 tsp salt and 1 tbsp lemon juice for 4-5 minutes till crisp tender. Strain and pat dry on a clean kitchen towel.
2. Break stem of chillies and tap gently to remove seeds. Dry roast all ingredients on a tawa for 2-3 minutes. Place the roasted spices with garlic, oil and lemon juice in a grinder and grind to a coarse paste. Remove to a flat dish. Add salt and marinate the potato fingers in the paste till serving time.
3. To serve, cover a grill rack with aluminium foil. Grease it with some oil. Place fingers on it. Sprinkle both cheeses on them. Grill the potatoes for about 10- 12 minutes or till they turn golden. Serve hot. If using paneer, grill for just 4-5 minutes.

Haryali Paneer Tikka

Serves 6

400 gm paneer - cut into 1½" long pieces, ¾" thick

4 tbsp yogurt - hang in a muslin cloth for 1 hour

4 tbsp gram flour (*besan*)

1 tsp salt, 4 tbsp oil

GRIND TO A CHUTNEY (FINE PASTE)

1 cup fresh green coriander (*hara dhania*)

1 green chilli - deseeded and chopped

2 tsp fennel (*saunf*)

½" piece ginger, 5-6 flakes garlic

½ tsp salt, 4 tbsp lemon juice

1. Grind together coriander, green chilli, fennel, ginger, garlic, salt and lemon juice to a fine chutney paste. Do not add water while grinding.
2. Slit the paneer pieces almost till the end and keep aside.
3. Divide the chutney into 2 parts.
4. With one part of the chutney, stuff some chutney in the slits of all the paneer pieces. Keep the stuffed paneer aside.
5. Heat 4 tbsp oil. Add gramflour and roast on low heat, till it turns fragrant. Do not make it brown. Let it cool.
6. Mix together the left over chutney with hung yogurt. Add salt and roasted gramflour. Rub this all over the stuffed paneer pieces.
7. Rub oil generously over the grill of the oven or wire rack of a gas tandoor. Place paneer on the greased wire rack or grill of the oven.
8. Heat an oven or a gas tandoor on moderate heat. Grill paneer for 7 minutes. Spoon some drops of oil on the paneer pieces in the oven or tandoor and grill further for 5 minutes. Serve hot.

Note: To cook the tikkas in the oven, cover the plate under the tray with aluminium foil, to collect the drippings that fall from the tikkas.

Mini Corn Buns

Makes 12

12 mini buns, soup buns may be used

2 tbsp olive oil mixed with ¼ tsp each of - salt, pepper, oregano

2 tbsp oil

1 onion - finely chopped

¾ cup chopped cabbage

½ red capsicum - cubed

½ cup frozen corn

1 cheese cube - cut into tiny pieces

½ cup tiny pieces of paneer

1 tbsp chopped coriander or 1 tsp chopped mint or parsley

MIX TOGETHER

3 tbsp mayonnaise

3 tbsp thick yogurt (hang ½ cup yogurt for 30 minutes)

2 tsp tomato ketchup

1 tsp mustard sauce/ chilli garlic spread

1. Hollow out the buns. Brush the outside and inside of each bun with olive oil mixed with spices. Keep aside.
2. Heat 2 tbsp olive oil or regular cooking oil in a pan Add onion and cook till soft. Add cabbage and cook for 3 minutes. Add red capsicum and corn. Mix well. Add ¾ tsp salt, ½ tsp pepper and ½ tsp oregano. Add coriander leaves, paneer and cheese. Mix well and keep aside.
3. Mix mayonnaise with thick yogurt, ketchup and chilli garlic spread or mustard.
4. Add vegetables to mayonnaise mix and check salt. Stuff in the buns and grill in a oven on the rack for 5 minutes till edges start to turn golden. Serve hot.

Mexican Canapes

Makes 8

8 monita's canapes or any salted biscuit

FILLING

4 baby corns - cut into thin long 1" pieces or ½ cup boiled corn

½ cup finely chopped french beans or capsicum

2 tbsp baked beans or boiled *rajmah*

2 tbsp olive oil

1 tsp chopped ginger

1 onion - finely chopped

½ tsp each of salt, red chilli flakes and oregano

3 tbsp salsa, available ready made

SOUR CREAM

½ cup yogurt - hang for 30 minutes

2 tbsp cream

salt and white pepper to taste

GARNISH

1" green spring onion or a strip of capsicum

1. Grill the empty canapes in a preheated oven for 2-3 minutes to turn crisp. Let cool and store in an air tight box 2-3 hours before serving.
2. Mix all the ingredients of sour cream. Check taste and refrigerate.
3. For the topping, heat olive oil. Add ginger and onion and stir till golden. Add capsicum/ french beans and baby corn. Stir for 2-3 minutes. Add baked beans or *rajmah*. Add red chilli flakes, salt and oregano. Add salsa. Remove from fire.
4. At serving time, fill warm mixture into the canapes. Dot with sour cream and salsa with a spoon. Garnish with a green coriander leaf.

Pizza Crackers

Makes 24

1 pizza base or pita bread

4 tbsp olive oil mixed ½ tsp each of red chilli flakes and oregano and 2 pinches salt

roasted pepper dip or salsa to serve, see section on dips

1. Cut the base horizontally into 2 rounds. Mix olive with salt, red chilli flakes and oregano. Brush both rounds on both sides with olive oil.
2. With a pizza cutter, cut into 12 wedges. Place on a rack and bake at 210°C for 6 minutes till crisp and golden. Remove and cool. Store in an air tight box.
3. Arrange crackers in a platter and serve with dips given on page 97.

Dough for Super Veggie Pizza

Makes 2-3

3 tsp active dry yeast, 3 cups all-purpose plain flour (*maida*)

1 tsp sugar, 1 tsp salt, 1 tsp olive oil

1. To make pizza dough, put ½ cup warm water in a bowl. Feel with a finger to see, it should not be too hot or too cold. Add yeast, salt and sugar to the warm water in the bowl. Mix gently. Cover cup nicely and keep aside covered and undisturbed for 10-15 minutes or till it becomes frothy.
2. Sift flour through a sieve into a bowl. Make a well in the centre and add the yeast mixture. Mix.
3. Knead to a smooth dough with enough warm water. Now oil your hands and knead well on a floured kitchen surface for about 10 minutes, or until smooth and elastic.
4. Put in a well greased large bowl and cover bowl for 15 minutes. Do not prove for more than 30 minutes as over proving is not good for the dough. You can refrigerate the dough incase you are not able to complete the pizza for any reason, though completing the pizza after the dough is ready, is really the best. (While the dough is being proved, you can make the sauce and topping).
5. Make a log of the dough and cut into 2-3 equal portions with a knife (2 for regular pizza and 3 for thin crust.) Take one ball. Keep remaining balls covered with an inverted bowl on top to prevent them from drying. Do not wrap in cling film.
6. Roll out the ball into a 7" round on a floured surface.
7. Grease a large (10-12") baking tray with olive oil. Preheat oven to 220°C.
8. Carefully pick up the rolled pizza and place on the greased baking pan. Now push the base outwards with your hands to get a 10-12" round, depending on the thickness you like.
9. Brush the base with olive oil. Prick pizza lightly with a fork. On the pizza base in the baking pan, put sauce, then most of the cheese, topping and finally a little cheese. Drizzle with olive oil. Bake for 8 minutes at 220°C, or until the sides and bottom are crisp and golden brown. Repeat with the remaining dough.

Super Veggie Pizza

Makes 2 pizzas

PIZZA BASE

recipe for 2 pizza base on page 28 or 2 ready made base

TOMATO SAUCE

3 tomatoes - blanched (put in hot water and peeled) and chopped finely

¼ cup ready made tomato puree, 4-5 flakes garlic - crushed

1 tsp dried oregano, ¾ tsp salt and ¼ tsp freshly ground pepper, or to taste, 1 tbsp oil

TOPPING

1 onion - cut into ½" pieces

½ cup small florets of broccoli - put in boiling water for a minute

½ red or yellow bell pepper - cut into ½" squares

½ cup tinned corn kernels or cooked fresh corn

a few slices of pickled jalapenos

a few sundried tomatoes and fresh basil leaves

10-15 olives - cut into slices

150 gms mozzarella or pizza cheese - grated

2 tbsp olive oil

¼ tsp salt, ¼ tsp red chilli flakes, ½ tsp oregano

1. Prepare the pizza base as given on page 28 or use 2 ready made bases.
2. To prepare the tomato sauce, heat oil in a pan. Add garlic. Stir and immediately add all other ingredients of the sauce. Bring to a boil. Lower heat and simmer on low heat for 10 minutes, till thick enough to spread without being runny.
3. Mix onions, coloured bell peppers and blanched broccoli with 1 tbsp olive oil, ¼ tsp salt, ½ tsp oregano and ¼ red chilli flakes.
4. Spoon tomato sauce over each pizza base, leaving ½" all around the edges. Brush the edges with olive oil. Sprinkle ¼ of the grated cheese on each base. Sprinkle vegetables. Sprinkle some corn and jalapenos too.
5. Sprinkle left over cheese. Arrange olives, basil & sundried tomatoes. Drizzle some olive oil. Bake on the wire rack of the oven at 220°C for 8 mins. until golden & crisp.

Calzone

During baking the calzone swells somewhat until it resembles a "stuffed stocking," the literal translation of the word calzone.

Makes 8

FILLING

3 tbsp butter

2 cups sliced mushroom

1 red capsicum - chopped

1 green capsicum - chopped

3 onions - sliced finely

2 tbsp chopped garlic

2 tbsp flour (*maida*)

1 cup milk

1 cup grated cheese

oregano and salt to taste

DOUGH

recipe of basic pizza dough given on page 28

1. Make pizza dough as given on page 28. Keep aside to prove.
2. For the filling, heat the butter in a sauce pan and sauté the onion and garlic for a minute. Add the mushroom and red and green capsicum and sauté for 2 minutes on high flame. Sprinkle the flour, cook for 30 seconds, add milk and let it come to a boil. Stir till thick. Add cheese oregano, salt and mix well and remove from fire. Cool the mixture.
3. Make 8 balls. Roll out one ball into a 6" circle. Put one part of the filling on the circle. Fold over to form a semi circle. Seal the ends with little water and press the edges firmly with the help of a fork.
4. Place on a greased baking tray. Cover and keep for 10 minutes. Bake in a pre-heated oven at 200°C for 15 minutes or until evenly browned.
5. Remove from the oven and brush with melted butter.

Baked Cheesy Nachos

Makes 4 tortillas (32 pieces)

¼ cups maize flour (*makai ka atta*)

¾ cup flour (*maida*), 2 pinches baking powder

2 tsp lemon juice

¼ tsp salt, ¼ tsp chilli powder

¼ tsp oregano, 2 tbsp oil

TO SERVE

some grated cheese

2 tbsp each of finely chopped tomato and onion

salsa, ready made, crushed black pepper

a few boiled kidney beans (*rajmah*)

a few jalapenos

SOUR CREAM

½ cup yogurt - hang for 15 minutes

2 tbsp cream

1 tsp lemon juice

salt and white pepper to taste

1. Mix maize flour, flour, baking powder, salt, red chilli powder and oregano in a big bowl. Add oil and lemon juice. Knead with warm water to make a pliable dough. Cover with a moist cloth and keep aside for 10 minutes.

2. Divide the dough into 4 balls. Roll into a shape of a very thin round chappati. Cut each tortilla into 8 wedges and bake at 230°C in a baking tray in a single layer for 6-7 minutes till crisp. Let them cool.

3. To serve, arrange 15-16 chips (store rest in an airtight container) in a single layer on a baking sheet or oven proof platter and sprinkle some cheese. Mix boiled beans with 2-3 tbsp salsa and scatter on the nachos. Scatter some onion, tomatoes and jalapenos too. Sprinkle grated cheese again. Sprinkle some pepper. Put in a hot oven for 2-3 minutes. Serve with salsa and sour cream.

Vegetable Quiche

Serves 4

BASE

1/3 cup melted butter, 1½ cups plain flour (*maida*)

4-5 tbsp cold water or as required

¼ cup grated cheddar cheese (25 gm)

QUICHE FILLING

½ cup cooked corn

1 small capsicum - chopped

1 onion - shredded

4-5 mushrooms - sliced

½ cup finely chopped carrots

¼ cup finely chopped beans

1 tbsp butter

½ cup mozzarella cheese

1 cup cheddar or ½ cup cheddar cheese and ½ cup paneer

5 tbsp thick cream, preferably Amul

5 tbsp tomato puree

1 tbsp cornflour

1 egg white, optional

½ tsp salt

¼ tsp pepper powder

½ tsp dried basil or ½ tsp dried oregano

1 medium tomato - sliced into thick rings and then cut each round into half

1. For the base, sift flour. Combine the butter and flour, rubbing well until it looks like bread crumbs. Add cheese to the mixture. Add just enough water to bind and gather lightly to a firm dough. Cover the dough and keep aside for 15 minutes in the fridge. Roll out the dough 1/8" thick, between 2 plastic sheets slightly bigger than the quiche tin. You can use a 9" loose bottom flan tin or small , about 4" individual quiche tins. Press the rolled out dough carefully in the tins to get a well levelled base. See that it is big enough to go upto the sides. Trim the excess on top by pressing on the sharp edge of the tin. Prick with a fork all over to avoid the crust from puffing up during baking. Put quiche shell in the freezer for 10 minutes.
2. Put the quiche crust on low rack in a preheated oven at 190°C. Bake for 12 minutes or until light golden brown. Allow to cool.
3. Heat 1 tbsp butter. Add sliced onions and cook till golden. Cook mushrooms for 2-3 min. Add beans and carrots. Stir for 2 minutes. Add capsicum and corn. Cook for a few seconds. Sprinkle ½ tsp salt. Remove from fire.
4. Mix together - cream, tomato puree, cornflour, salt, pepper, oregano or basil. Add 1 eggwhite if using. Beat well and keep aside.
5. Spoon corn-vegetable mixture into the cooled quiche crust, level it.
6. Sprinkle most of the grated cheese on it, keeping some for the top.
7. Spread the cream mixture on the cheese. Press the slices of tomato on top, sprinkle with the remaining cheese. Sprinkle some oregano or crushed peppercorns.
8. Drizzle with olive oil. Put the quiche on low rack in the oven. Bake at 180°C for 10 minutes or until the filling is set and the top is golden. Allow to cool before slicing.

Steamed Momos

Makes 12

DOUGH

¾ cup plain flour (*maida*)

¼ cup rice flour or cornflour

1 tbsp oil, ½ tsp salt

FILLING

1 onion - finely chopped, 6 mushrooms - chopped very finely

1 tsp ginger-garlic paste

2 green chillies - finely chopped

1 large carrot - very finely chopped or grated

2½ cups very finely chopped cabbage (1 small cabbage)

1 tsp salt and ½ tsp pepper powder, or to taste

1 tbsp vinegar, ½ tsp soya sauce

RED HOT CHUTNEY

1 tsp ginger chopped, 1 tbsp chopped garlic flakes

8-10 dry red chillies - break into pieces and soak in hot water for 10 minutes

1 tsp cumin seeds, 2 tbsp oil

2 tsp sugar, ¾ tsp salt

2 tbsp tomato ketchup

½ tsp soya sauce, 1 tsp vinegar, or to taste

1. Sift flour with salt. Add oil and knead with enough water to make a stiff dough of rolling consistency, as that for puris. Keep in a cool place covered with a damp cloth for 30 minutes.
2. Heat 2 tbsp oil in the *kadhai* for the filling. Add the chopped onion. Fry till it turns soft. Add mushrooms and cook further for 2 minutes. Add green chillies, carrot and ginger-garlic paste. Mix well and add the cabbage. Stir fry on high flame for 3 minutes. Add salt, pepper, vinegar and soya sauce to taste. Remove from fire and keep the filling aside to cool.

3. Take out the dough and form marble sized small balls. Roll out flat, as thin as possible into small rounds of 2½" diameter.
4. Put 1 heaped tsp of the filling on one side and fold over to form a semicircle. Stick the edges with water.
5. Pleat the joint edges and then slightly fold the pointed ends to give it a little rounded shape. Make all momos. Keep aside.
6. To steam, place the momos in a greased steamer or in an idli stand or in a greased colander (steel *channi* with big holes) and steam for 10 minutes.
7. For chutney, grind the soaked red chillies along with ginger, garlic, cumin seeds, oil, salt and sugar to a paste. Add tomato ketchup, soya sauce and vinegar to taste.

STEP 3

STEP 4

STEP 5

STEP 6

Mushroom Olive Rolls

Serves 3-4

6 slices of white bread

mayonnaise - enough to spread

***maida* paste (1 tbsp *maida* mixed with 2 tbsp water) - to seal**

1 tsp onion seeds (*kalaunji*) mixed with 3 tsp white sesame seeds

FILLING

1 tbsp oil

1 cup roughly chopped mushrooms, ½ red bell pepper - chopped

1 tbsp chopped olives

½ onion - finely chopped, 1 tsp finely chopped garlic

1 tsp deseeded and chopped green chillies

2 tbsp chopped fresh coriander

1 tbsp grated cheddar cheese, 1 tbsp grated mozarella cheese

½ tsp salt, pepper to taste

1. To prepare the filling, heat oil. Add garlic, green chillies and onion cook for a few minutes till soft. Add mushrooms and stir for 3 minutes, add red bell pepper and olives. Remove from fire. Add all the remaining ingredients of the filling and mix well.
2. Cut sides of bread. Warm each slice in the microwave for 10 seconds. Immediately with a rolling pin, roll out a slice with pressure to make it thin. Roll out the second slice also quickly. Now place one slice on the kitchen platform and place the second one slightly overlapping the first one. With a rolling pin, press on the joint to seal.
3. Join 2 rolled out slices using flour paste to get a long piece of bread. Roll out the whole bread again. Spread mayonnaise on the slices.
4. Put 1/3 of the filling at one end and roll up. Seal the end with flour paste.
5. With a butter knife, spread mayonnaise on the roll on all sides. Roll over sesame seeds mixed with onion seeds.
6. Preheat grill for 5-10 minutes. Cover rack with foil. Place rolls on it and put under the grill for 7 minutes, turn and grill for 2-3 minutes till golden and crisp. Cut each into 3 pieces with a sharp bread knife.

Pinwheels with Roasted Peppers

Enjoy it plain or grilled.

Serves 12

8 slices of white bread or 2-3 flour tortillas

12 spinach leaves or bunch of fresh lettuce leaves

½ cup ordinary (permal) rice

2 tbsp sweet chilli sauce (thin, translucent sauce for spring rolls)

1 large red capsicum

1 tbsp olive oil

2 pinches of salt

½ tsp red chilli flakes

YOGURT SPREAD

1 cup yogurt - hang for 30 minutes

1 tsp mixed herbs

½ tsp salt, a pinch powdered sugar

1 tsp mustard sauce

2 drops lemon juice

2 tsp extra virgin olive oil

1. Wash rice. Put in a pressure cooker with ¼ tsp salt and ¾ cups water. Keep on fire. Allow 2 whistles. Remove from fire and let the pressure drop by itself.
2. If using spinach, wash spinach leaves and spread them on a microproof plate. Cover with a wrap and microwave for 30 seconds.
3. Roast the red pepper on naked flame till nicely black all over to get a smoky flavour. Remove from fire and cover immediately to trap the smoky flavour. After 10 minutes, peel and cut into very small pieces.
4. Mix hung yogurt with all ingredients with a whisk till smooth. Keep aside.
5. Mix ½ cup cooked rice with 2 tbsp sweet chilli sauce. Add smoked and chopped red peppers. Keep aside.
6. If using, bread, cut the sides of slices nicely from all sides. Place 2 slices in the microwave on the turn table and microwave for 10 seconds. Remove from microwave.

7. Immediately with a rolling pin, roll out a slice with pressure to make it thin. Roll out the second slice also quickly. Now place one slice on the kitchen platform and place the second one slightly overlapping the first one. With a rolling pin, press on the joint to seal. Roll out the whole bread again.
8. Spread 1-2 tsp of the mustard yogurt on the rolled out bread or a tortilla.
9. Place 3 blanched spinach leaves one above the other widthwise, on the bread so as to cover the bread. Use a big lettuce leaf if you like.
10. Spread a thin layer of prepared rice with peppers on it.
11. Carefully roll to make a firm cylinder. Keep with the joint side down for 5 minutes to secure. You can serve it plain or grill in the oven. To grill, brush roll with olive oil and sprinkle some chilli flakes. Grill in a preheated oven for 5-8 minutes. Cut into pieces with a bread knife.
12. Thin down the remaining yogurt with some olive oil or water and serve as a dip with the rolls.

Baked Pyaz ki Kachori

Makes 8 kachoris

DOUGH

1½ cups plain flour (*maida*)

5 tbsp melted ghee

¾ tsp baking powder, ½ tsp salt

ONION FILLING

2 tbsp oil, 2 cups finely chopped onions

1 tsp nigella seeds (*kalaunji*)

2 tsp fennel seeds (*saunf*)

1 bay leaf (*tej patta*)

2 green chillies - chopped

2 tbsp gram flour (*besan*)

2 tsp coriander (*dhania*) powder

2 tsp chilli powder

1 tsp garam masala

3 tbsp chopped coriander, salt to taste

1. Knead all ingredients of the dough into a semi-soft dough using about ½ cup water. Knead well for 5-7 minutes.
2. For filling, heat oil. Add nigella seeds and fennel. After a few seconds, add bay leaf, green chillies and onions. Stir for 3- 4 minutes till onions turn light brown. Reduce heat. Add gramflour and remaining ingredients and cook for 2 minutes. Remove bay leaf. Cool.
3. Roll a ball of the dough into a 2½" circle. Place filling. Cover with the dough. Seal the ends tightly. Roll out into a 3" diameter circle.
4. Bake the kachoris in a preheated oven at 200°C for 15-20 minutes till golden.

Party Snacks in Minutes

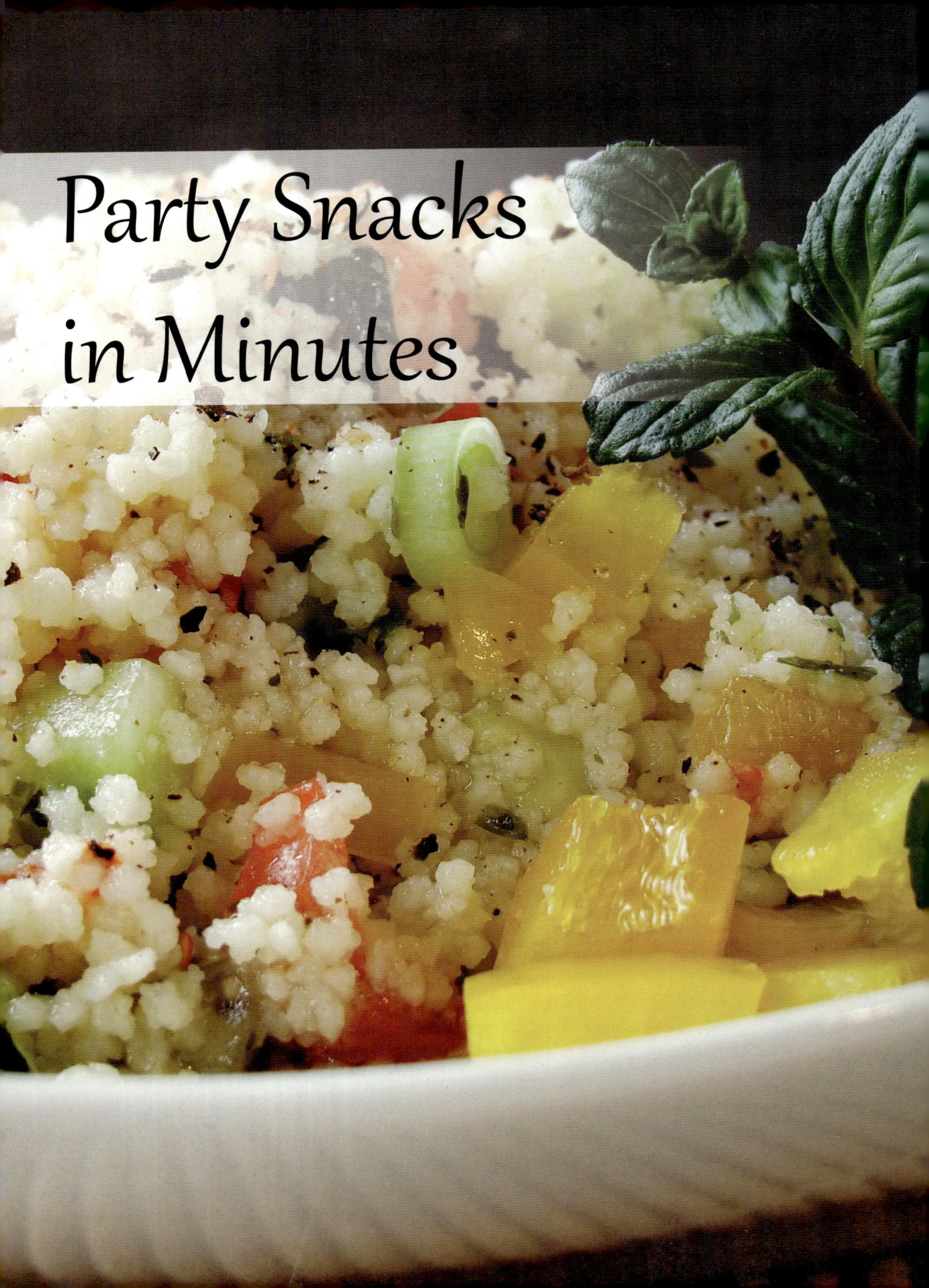

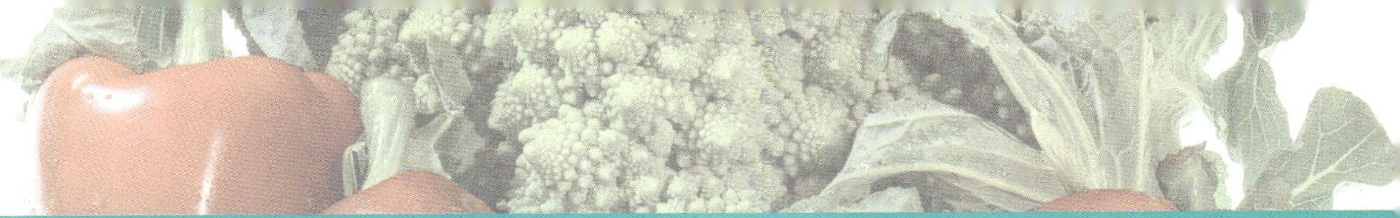

Semolina Fillets

Makes15-20

1 cup semolina (*suji*)

3 tbsp olive oil

1 green chilli - chopped

½ cup finely chopped broccoli or french beans

½ cup finely chopped red capsicum

1½ cups milk

½ tsp each of oregano, red chilli flakes

1½ tsp salt, ¼ tsp crushed black pepper

2 tbsp chopped fresh basil leaves or coriander

¼ cup corn

50 gms paneer - grated

COATING

1½ cups crushed cornflakes mixed with 1 tbsp oil and ½ tsp red chilli flakes

2 tbsp flour (*maida*) mixed with ¼ cup water

1. Heat 3 tbsp oil. Add green chillies and stir. Add broccoli and stir for 2 minutes. Add red capsicum and ¼ tsp of salt.
2. Add milk and stir to combine.
3. Sprinkle semolina gradually, stirring with the other hand till well mixed. Stir till thick. Add 1¼ tsp salt, red chilli flakes, oregano and pepper. Add fresh basil/coriander and corn. Stir till very thick and forms a lump.
4. Remove from fire and add paneer. Mix well.
5. Transfer to a greased flat surface and shape into ½" thick block. Let it set for 15 minutes. Neaten edges and cut into 1" squares.
6. Dip in a thin flour batter and roll over seasoned cornflakes. Bake in a hot oven at 200°C for 20 minutes or till golden.

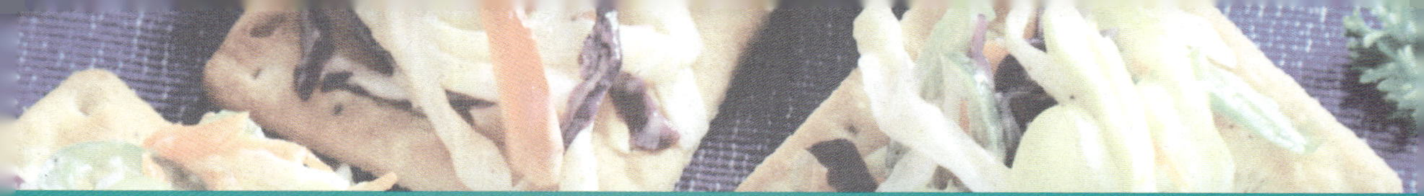

Coleslaw Canapes

Makes 9

9 veggie crackers (salted biscuits)

4 tbsp mayonnaise mixed with 1 tsp hot & sweet tomato sauce and ½ tsp mustard sauce

2 tbsp each of finely shredded cabbage

2 tbsp shredded green capsicum

2 tbsp shredded red cabbage or grated carrot, a few grapes

1. Mix mayonnaise with tomato sauce and mustard. Add the vegetables and mix. Add salt and pepper to taste. Refrigerate till serving time.
2. To serve, pile on crackers or bread and top with a grape half. Serve.

Corn & Paneer Chaat

Serve 2-3

1 cup frozen corn kernels, see note
1 tbsp softened butter
1 onion - chopped finely
1 tomato - chopped
1 tbsp finely chopped coriander
1-2 green chillies - chooped
50 gms paneer - cut into tiny cubes
½ tsp black salt
½ tsp chaat masala
½ tsp black pepper
salt to taste
1 tsp lemon juice, or to taste

1. Put corns in 1 cup water and microwave for 2-3 minutes. Alternately, put corns in boiling water for a minute. Strain corn kernels and put in a bowl. Mix butter with the hot corn.
2. Add all the other ingredients along with paneer and mix. Garnish with coriander leaves.

Note: you can boil fresh corn kernels also.

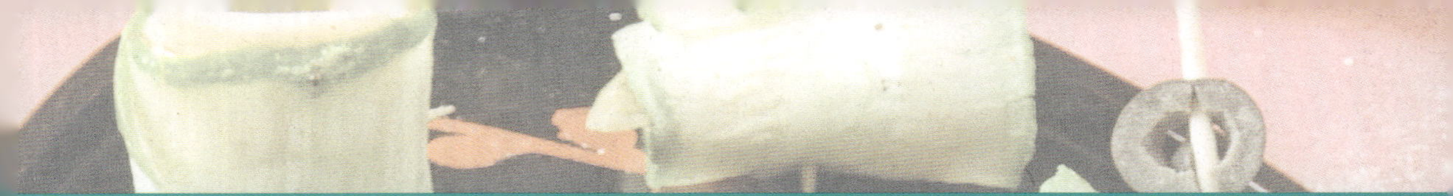

Cucumber Rolls

A cold snack!

Serves 8-10

1 thick large green cucumber (*kheera*) - peel with a peeler from all 4 sides, leaving the centre seedy part

1-2 tsp mango chutney or any other similar chutney

3-4 cheese slices

8-10 jalapeno slices

8-10 sliced black olives

a few tooth picks

1. Place a cucumber peel on a flat surface or a chopping board. Place another one slightly over lapping it.
2. Spread just about 1/8 tsp mango chutney on the slice. (The rolls should not taste sweet).
3. Cut a cheese slice into 3 pieces. Place one piece over the cucumber.
4. Place a whole big jalapeno slice and top with a sliced black olive.
5. Roll the cucumber peel and secure with a tooth pick.
6. Place on a serving platter and loosely cover with a wrap or keep in a box and refrigerate till serving time.

Pasta Bites

Serves 4

¾ cup big, roundish pasta

2 tbsp grated cheese

2 tinned pineapple slices - each cut into ½" pieces

a few thick slices of black olives

tooth picks

TOMATO SAUCE

1 tsp oil

2-3 flakes of garlic - crushed to a paste (1 tsp)

4 tbsp ready made tomato puree

1 tbsp tomato ketchup

¼ tsp salt

½ tsp each of oregano and red chilli flakes

1. To boil pasta, boil 3 cups water with ½ tsp salt and 1 tsp oil. Add pasta to boiling water. Stir to see that pasta is not sticking to the bottom of the pan. Boil, stirring occasionally, for about 8 minutes till pasta turns almost soft, but yet firm. Do not overcook. Remove from fire and leave pasta in hot water for 2 minutes. Strain. Leave for 2 minutes in strainer for all water to drain out.
2. In the meanwhile, prepare the tomato sauce, heat oil. Add garlic. Stir and add tomato puree, tomato ketchup, oregano, and salt. Cook for 2-3 minutes on medium heat. Remove from heat. Add pasta and cheese. Mix well to coat. Keep aside covered till serving time.
3. To serve, thread a pasta, then a small piece of pineapple and then an olive on a tooth pick.

Mustard & Corn Slice

Makes 16

4 slices of multigrain bread - lightly toasted

1 cup finely chopped spinach

1 cup (½ tin) cream style sweet corn

¼ cup whole corn kernels, frozen or boiled

1 tbsp butter, 1 tsp chopped garlic

4 tbsp milk

1 green chilli - finely chopped

½ tsp pepper powder, salt to taste

2 pinches of baking powder

2 tbsp mustard sauce to spread

4 tbsp (1 cube) grated cheese

1. Heat butter, add garlic. Stir for a few seconds and add spinach. Cook till dry. Add cream style corn, milk, green chillies, pepper and salt. Stir and simmer till the liquid is absorbed. Add whole corn kernels also. Mix well. Remove from heat. Add baking powder.
2. Spread mustard on the lightly toasted bread.
3. Apply the mixture over bread pieces, top with grated cheese and grill for 5 minutes. Cut into 4 small squares or triangles to serve.

Hot Cheese Fondue

Serves 6-8

1½ cups grated cheddar cheese

½ cup milk

½ tsp white pepper powder

½ tsp dried oregano

½ tsp dried thyme

1. Heat the cheese and milk together in a double boiler, or in a heat-proof bowl placed on a pan of simmering water to make a double boiler. Stir continuously for about 7-8 minutes till the cheese melts and the mixture is smooth.
2. Season with salt, pepper and dried herbs.
3. Serve immediately with crudites (cut raw vegetables), wafers or bread sticks.

Chef's Tip: This dip tastes best when hot as the cheese solidifies when cold. To reheat, microwave on low power (300-400) for 20-30 seconds. Keep a watch, it boils over very fast.

Peanut Butter Cracker Sandwich

Serves 2/Makes 4

8 cream crackers or veggie crackers (biscuits)

2 cheese slices - each cut into 4 pieces

MIX TOGETHER

2 tbsp cheese spread

2 tbsp crunchy peanut butter

1 tbsp tomato ketchup

¼ tsp pepper

¼ tsp oregano

2 tbsp milk

a pinch of salt

1. Mix all ingredients in a bowl to create a spread.
2. Spread on 4 biscuits. Keep a square piece of cheese slice. Cover with the remaining biscuits to form a diamond. Serve.

Broccoli Peanut Kebab

Makes-6-8

200 gms broccoli (1 small flower) - chopped finely along with tender stalks (1½ cups)

1 onion - chopped finely

¼ cup roasted peanuts - crushed coarsely with a rolling pin (*belan*)

1 tbsp oil

OAT SAUCE

2 tbsp oil

¼ cup oats

¾ cup milk

½ tsp salt and ¼ tsp pepper, or to taste

1. Break broccoli into florets and wash well. Chop the broccoli florets and the tender stems finely.
2. Heat 1 tbsp oil in a pan. Add onion and saute for a minute. Add broccoli and 2 pinches of salt and stir on low heat for 2-3 minutes till slightly tender. Remove from heat.
3. Add peanuts to broccoli and keep aside.
4. For the oat sauce, heat 2 tbsp oil and add oats. Stir for a few minutes and remove from heat. Add milk. Mix well and return to heat. Stir on medium heat till thick. Cook till the sauce thickens and starts leaving the sides of the pan.
5. Add salt, pepper and broccoli to the oat mixture. Cook further for 2 minutes on low heat. Remove from heat and cool completely. If in a hurry, refrigerate the mixture so that it becomes firm enough to handle.
6. Make round kebabs, keeping them a little thick. Fry in a pan lightly brushed with oil. Turn sides to brown both sides lightly. Serve.

Masala Papad

Do everything just before serving for a quick crisp snack.

Serves 2

2 medium sized papads (roasting ones)

TOPPING

¼ cup finely chopped cucumber

¼ cup finely chopped tomato

¼ cup finely chopped onion

¼ cup very finely chopped paneer

2 tbsp finely chopped coriander

1 green chilli - deseeded and chopped finely

¼ tsp salt and red chilli powder, or to taste

½ tsp chaat masala or to taste

1-2 tsp lemon juice or to taste

1. Roast both papads and keep aside.
2. Mix all ingredients of topping. Check seasonings.
3. At serving time, spread a thin layer of topping on the roasted papad. Serve immediately.

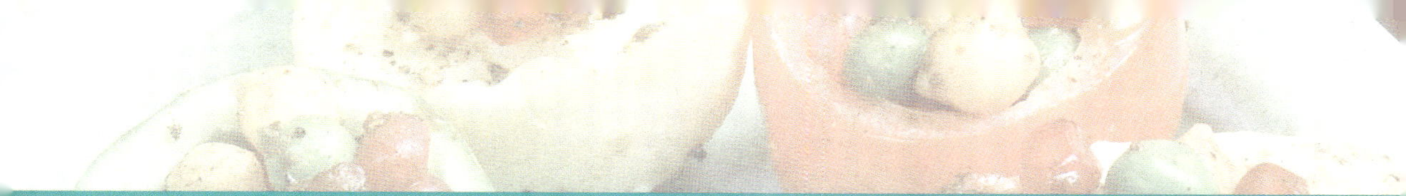

Fruit Kulle

Hollowed cups of vegetables are filled with chanas.

Serves 6

1 cucumber (*kheera*) - cut into 6 pieces, each about 1½" long

3 small potatoes - boiled, 3 small tomatoes

FILLING

½ cup chickpeas (*safed channa*) - soak in warm water for 5-6 hours

½ cup fresh pomegranate kernels (*anaar ke daane*)

½ cup grapes (use black or green) - each cut into half from the middle

½ cup peas - boiled

2-3 green chillies - deseeded and chopped

1 tsp chaat masala, preferably kala chaat masala

½ tsp roasted cumin powder (*bhuna jeera*)

juice of ½ lemon, salt to taste

1. Drain chickpeas. Put them in a pressure cooker with 1 tsp salt and 1 cup water. Pressure cook to give 2 whistles. Remove from fire. Strain chickpeas after pressure drops. Leave them in strainer for all the water to drain out.

2. Cut the cucumber into 6 pieces (1½" long) and scoop out the filling with a knife or scooper, keeping the base intact, to get hollow cups. Sprinkle some lemon juice and chat masala in the cups. Rub well.

3. Peel boiled potatoes. Cut each potato into 2 halves widthwise. Scoop out each piece with help of a scooper or knife to get hollow cups. Sprinkle some lemon juice and chat masala in potato cups and rub well. Keep aside. Similarly scoop out the tomato pieces with a knife or scooper, keeping the base intact. Sprinkle some lemon juice and chaat masala in tomato cups and rub well. Keep aside.

4. For filling, mix all ingredients with the boiled channas in a bowl. Check the filling and make it to your taste. Keep aside.

5. Fill each hollowed vegetable with this filling, heaping it a little. Serve.

Dakshini Squares

Snack with a South Indian touch.

Serves 4

75 gms paneer - crumbled (¾ cup)

2 tbsp semolina (*suji*)

½ tsp salt, or to taste

¼ tsp pepper, or to taste

½ onion - very finely chopped

2 tbsp curry leaves

½ tomato - cut into half, deseeded and chopped finely

3 multigrain bread slices - toasted in a toaster

½ tsp brown mustard seeds (*rai*)

3 tsp oil to shallow fry

1. Mix the semolina, salt and pepper with the paneer using your fingers.
2. Add the onion, tomato and curry leaves.
3. Spread paneer mixture carefully on toasted bread slices, keeping edges neat.
4. Sprinkle some mustard seeds over the paneer mixture, pressing down gently with finger tips.
5. Heat 1 tsp oil in a non stick pan. Add a slice of bread with topping side down.
6. Cook until the topping turns golden brown and crisp. Add a little more oil for the next slice if required. Cut each slice into 4 pieces and serve hot.

Note: This recipe will work best using a minimum quantity of oil for frying.

Fruity Cottage Cheese Canapes

The combination of fruits and cottage cheese tastes divine!

Serves 6-8

sliced strawberry, black or green grapes, etc

a few mint leaves - dipped in water

BREAD CANAPES

8 slices white, brown, garlic bread (any bread of your choice)

1 tsp butter

SPREAD

½ cup mashed paneer, preferably home made

¾ cup thick curd (should not be sour)

1-2 flakes garlic - crushed (optional)

1 tbsp chopped mint

½ tsp mustard paste or powder

¼ tsp pepper powder, ¼ tsp salt, or to taste

1. To make canapes, press a fancy biscuit cutter or any round cap on a bread slice to get 2 canapes from each slice. (Kulfi mould cap makes an excellent canape cutter). If a biscuit cutter is not available, cut slices into 2 halves.
2. Butter the canape very lightly on one side. Heat oven to 210°C and bake the canapes for 5-7 minutes or till crisp. Cool canapes on a large tray (they should not overlap). Store in an air tight container. Canape bases can be made 2-3 days ahead.
3. For the spread, blend the paneer to a smooth paste with hung yogurt in a mixer.
4. Add all the other ingredients to the cottage cheese mixture. Mix well to make a spread and chill.
5. At serving time, spread cottage cheese generously on bread canapes and garnish with slices of varied fresh or tinned fruits and a mint leaf, making the canapes as varied and attractive as you can with your imagination.

Couscous Salad with Mint n Poppy Seeds Dressing

A sensational salad of coucous flavoured with paprika, with a crunchy "khus-khus" dressing.

serves 1

½ cup couscous
½ tsp salt
½ tsp paprika
2 tbsp chopped carrot
2 tbsp chopped red/yellow bell peppers
2 tbsp finely chopped beans/asparagus
8-10 pinenuts roasted

POPPY SEEDS DRESSING

1 tsp poppyseeds (*khus khus*)
1 tsp olive oil
1 tsp mint paste/chutney
2 tbsp mayonnaise

1. Boil 1 cup water. Add salt and paprika. Add couscous, stir and bring to a boil. Remove from fire and cover and keep aside for 10-15 minutes till water is absorbed.
2. If using asparagus, cut the top part of asparagus, about 3-4" long, and cut the lower bottom into thin pieces (chopped). Keep a few beans whole and chop the rest in the same way.
3. Heat 1 tbsp olive oil, add long asparagus stalks or whole beans, and saute on low heat till black patches appear. Remove from pan and keep aside for topping. Add the chopped, beans/ asparagus, carrots and bell peppers to the pan with ½ tbsp oil and saute for 2-3 minutes on low heat till soft. Add these chopped vegetables to the couscous.
4. Heat 1 tsp olive oil. Add 1 tsp khus khus and roast till golden and crisp. Transfer to a bowl. Add mint chutney/paste and mayonnaise.
5. In a serving platter, place a heap of couscous on one side. With a spoon, swirl the mint-mayo dressing on the couscous. Toss lightly with a fork. Top couscous with long sticks of asparagus or beans. Top with pinenuts. Garnish with fresh mint and serve.

Snacks from the Pan

Vegetable Shikampuri Kebab

Makes 12

1 cup chopped carrots - boiled, ½ cup chopped beans - boiled

½ cup chopped cauliflower - boiled, 4 potatoes - boiled and grated

4 tsp oil

2 green chillies - chopped finely, 1 tsp finely chopped ginger

½ tsp turmeric (*haldi*), 2 tsp chilli powder

1 tbsp chopped coriander, 1 tbsp chopped mint

salt to taste

2 fresh bread slices - grind in a mixer to get fresh bread crumbs

FLAVOURING POWDER (CRUSH TOGETHER)

1 tsp cumin seeds (*jeera*), 4 green cardamoms (*chhoti elaichi*)

2-3 pepper corns (*saboot kali mirch*), 2-3 cloves (*laung*)

2 blades mace (*javitri*) and ½ tsp carom seeds (*ajwain*)

FILLING

¼ cup grated paneer, ¼ cup yogurt - hang for 20 minutes in a muslin cloth

1 onion - chopped, ¼ cup khoya mashed

1 tbsp chopped mint, ¼ tsp salt, or to taste

1. Heat oil in a *kadhai*, add ginger and green chillies. Let ginger turn golden. Add carrots, beans, cauliflower. Stir fry for 2 minutes. Add turmeric and chilli powder. Stir for a few seconds.
2. Add grated potatoes and mix well. Add salt, coriander and mint leaves. Add flavouring powder. Cook for about 5 minutes till the mixture is well blended. Remove from heat.
3. Add enough bread crumbs to make firm round balls. Check salt and spices.
4. For the filling, brown the chopped onions in 1 tbsp oil on low heat. Remove from heat and let it cool. Add all other ingredients of the filling and mix well.
5. Flatten balls, stuff filling and shape into kebabs. Keep in the fridge for sometime to set well. Shallow fry in a pan in 2-3 tbsp oil till crisp and golden brown. Sprinkle some chaat masala on the hot kebabs and serve.

Mushroom Skewers

Makes 6-7

200 gms (10-12) small mushrooms - remove the stalk carefully and keep whole
¼ of red or green capsicum - cut into ½" pieces (6-7 pieces)
a few medium wooden skewers

MARINADE

2 tbsp soya sauce, 1 tsp grated ginger, 1 tsp crushed garlic
rind of 1 lemon, 1 tsp lemon juice, 1 tsp brown sugar or gur, 1 tbsp oil
¼ tsp red chilli flakes, ¼ tsp salt, 1 tsp ground cumin (*jeera powder*)

1. Mix all ingredients of the marinade together in a bowl.
2. Trim the mushroom stalks. Add mushroom caps, stalks and capsicum to the marinade and leave aside for at least one hour in the marinade. You can leave longer if you like.
3. At serving time, on a wooden stick, thread a mushroom cap side ways, keeping it flat, then a stalk, again a mushroom and a stalk. Finally top with a small piece of capsicum.
4. Heat 1-2 tbsp oil in a large non stick pan to grease the bottom of the pan. Put the skewers on it. Press lightly. Reduce heat. When the underside turns brown after 2-3 minutes, turn the side. Brown the other side also on low heat for 2-3 minutes. Spoon any left over marinade on the skewers. Remove from pan and serve hot.

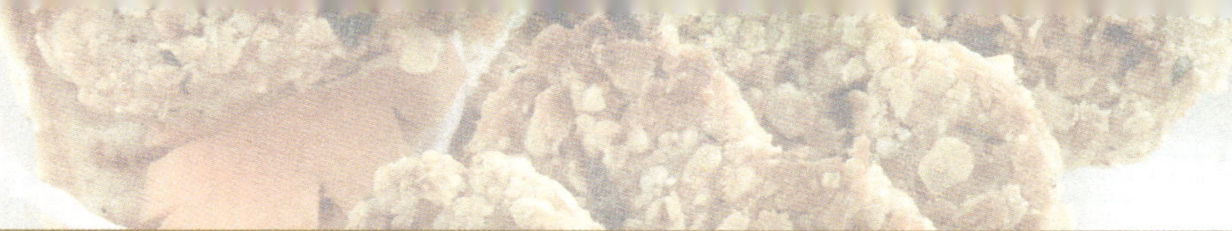

OAT HEARTS

Serves 3-4

1½ cups oats, 2 potatoes - boiled and mashed

1 tbsp oil, 1 tsp chopped ginger, 1 green chilli - chopped

¼ cup grated carrot, ¼ cup boiled peas

¼ cup grated paneer, 1 tsp tomato ketchup

¾ tsp salt or to taste, ¼ tsp red chilli powder, ¼ tsp garam masala

½ tsp dry mango powder (*amchoor*), 2 tbsp chopped coriander

1. Keep ½ cup oats aside for coating. Heat 1 tbsp oil. Add chopped ginger and green chilli. Stir and add carrot and peas. Stir for a minute. Add 1 cup oats. Stir for 2 minutes on low heat. Add potatoes and other ingredients and stir fry for 2-3 minutes. Add more ketchupas per your taste. Remove from fire and let it cool down.
2. Make 8-10 balls of the above mixture. Flatten each ball and shape into hearts or cut with a heart shape cookie cutter. Flatten slightly.
3. Spread the remaining ½ cup oats on a plate. Dip each heart in a bowl of water for a second and immediately press both sides of each heart in oats. Cook on a lightly greased non stick tawa till golden.

Herbed Potatoes

Serves 8

500 gm (3 large) potatoes - peeled and scooped to form balls (about 36 balls) or 30-35 baby potatoes (300 gm) - peeled

4 cups water, 1 tbsp lemon juice, 2 tsp salt

1 tbsp butler, 1 tbsp oil

1 tsp grated garlic

¾ tsp black pepper crushed

3 tbsp tomato ketchup, 1 tsp tamarind pulp (*imli*)

¼-½ tsp dried rosemary

¾ cup chopped fresh mixed herbs (basil//mint/coriander), use a combination of any 2-3 fresh herbs that are available

3 tsp finely crushed peanuts

2 tsp toasted sesame seeds

1. Peel the potatoes. Take out balls and prick with a fork. Boil 5 cups water with 1 tbsp lemon juice and 2 tsp salt. Add potatoes and boil in salted water for 7-8 minutes, or till they get cooked. Check with a knife to see that it goes inside smoothly without any resistance. Drain. Spread on a plate and cool potatoes.
2. Heat oil and butter in a medium non stick pan. Saute the potatoes, turning sides, for 7-8 minutes till golden. Remove from pan.
3. Heat remaining oil (1 tbsp) in the same pan. Reduce heat. Add garlic. Stir and add crushed pepper.
4. Add tomato ketchup and tamarind pulp. Stir and add dry rosemary. Stir.
5. Add fresh mixed herbs and stir to mix. Add potatoes. Saute to combine well. Check salt and add a pinch of salt or to taste.
6. Sprinkle finely crushed peanuts and mix well. Sprinkle sesame seeds and mix lightly. Remove from pan and serve on tooth picks.

Vegetable Satay with Peanut Sauce

Makes 12 Skewers

200 gms tofu or paneer - cubed to get 1½ " squares

200 gms mushrooms - remove the stalk completely and keep whole if small

12-15 slices, ¼" thick, zucchini, some cherry tomatoes

MARINADE

½ tsp salt, rind of 1 lemon, 2 tsp brown sugar or gur

2 tsp red curry paste or red chilli garlic spread, both available ready made

2 tbsp coconut milk

½ tsp soya sauce, ½" piece of ginger - grated (1 tsp)

1 tsp lemon juice, 1 tbsp cornflour, 4 flakes garlic - crushed to a paste (1 tsp)

½ tsp cumin powder (*jeera*), ½ tsp coriander powder (*dhania*)

PEANUT SAUCE

¼ cup roasted salted peanuts, ½ onion - chopped

½ tsp salt, ½ tsp red chilli powder, 1 tbsp oil, ½ -1 tsp sugar, 1 tsp coriander powder (*dhania*)

1 tsp cumin powder (*jeera*), 4-6 flakes garlic - crushed (1 tsp)

1½ tsp lemon juice, 1 tsp soya sauce, ½-¾ cup ready-made coconut milk

1. Boil 3 cups water in a pan, add mushrooms in it. Boil for 2-3 minutes. Remove from fire, strain and refresh in cold water.
2. Mix all ingredients of marinade together in a flat dish. Mix paneer, mushrooms, zucchini and tomatoes nicely in the marinade.
3. Thread all onto wooden skewers.
4. Put the ready skewers in a flat dish (not bowl). Pour the remaining marinade over it, if any. Turn each skewer gently to coat. Cover and keep aside.
5. To make peanut sauce, grind peanuts with all ingredients with enough coconut milk to get a thick sauce.
6. To serve, heat 2 tbsp oil in a pan. Put the skewers on it. When the underside gets done turn the side. Do not turn till you get a nice brown colour. Brown the other side also. Serve peanut sauce with satay.

Paneer Shashlik

Serves 8-10

500 gm paneer - cut into 1½" squares of ½" thickness

2-3 tbsp oil, 2 capsicums - cut into ¾" squares

MARINADE

½ cup thick curd - hang for 20 minutes to drain the water, 4 tbsp cream

1 tsp lemon juice, 1 tsp tandoori masala, ¾ tsp chat masala, ½ tsp red chilli powder

½ tsp black salt (*kala namak*), ¼ tsp turmeric (*haldi*) powder, salt to taste

1. Mix hung curd with all the other ingredients of the marinade and marinate paneer in it. Keep aside in the fridge till serving time.
2. At the time of serving, heat a non-stick tawa. Spread 2 tbsp oil on the tawa. Place the marinated paneer pieces one by one on the tawa (they should not overlap). Cook on both sides for 1-2 minutes till masala slightly coats the paneer pieces (over cooking hardens paneer). Remove to a serving platter.
3. Toss capsicum pieces on the tawa. Saute and sprinkle chat masala.
4. Place one capsicum piece on each paneer. Pierce both with a toothpick and serve hot.

Bhutte Ki Seekh

Makes 15 pieces

2 cups frozen corn kernels - keeping aside 1 cup whole, roughly grind the remaining 1 cup corns in mixer

½ cup gram flour (*besan*)

1 tsp turmeric powder (*haldi*)

1 cup finely grated paneer

2 tbsp melted butter

3 tbsp finely chopped green chillies

¼ cup chopped green coriander

2 tsp chopped ginger

2 tsp degi mirch powder, 2 tsp garam masala powder

2 tsp chaat masala, 2 tsp tandoori masala

1¼ tsp salt, or to taste

1. Put the roughly ground corn in a muslin cloth and squeeze well till dry.
2. Dry roast gram flour on a *tawa* or in a *kadhai* along with turmeric powder for 2-3 minutes on medium flame till golden brown.
3. In a bowl place grated paneer and squeezed corn. Mix well. Add all the other ingredients and mix with the palm, binding the mixture nicely. Check seasonings and keep aside in the fridge to cool and become firm.
4. Divide mixture into equal balls and give them a seekh kabab shape by using a skewer. Take out from skewer. Pan fry 2-3 kebabs at a time in a non stick pan in 1-2 tbsp oil till brown from all sides.
5. Serve with onion rings mixed with a little green chutney and chaat masala.

Cottage Cheese Shooters

Serves 8

200 gm paneer (use tetra pack) - cut into fingers

a few satay/bamboo sticks

MIX TOGETHER

1 tsp soya sauce

2 tbsp olive oil

2 tsp ginger-garlic paste

2 tbsp stir fry sauce

1 tbsp tomato ketchup

1 tsp chilli - garlic spread

¼ tsp salt n pepper

½ tsp red chilli flakes

2 tsp cornflour

1 tsp vinegar, optional

1 tsp honey, optional

COATING

1½ cups cornflakes - crushed in a mixer to form crumbs

2 tbsp white sesame seeds, 2 tsp black sesame seeds, optional

1. Mix soya sauce with all ingredients in a bowl. Keep sauces aside.
2. Cut paneer and pat dry and keep aside in the fridge.
3. Mix cornflakes crumbs with both sesame seeds. Keep aside.
4. To serve, dip a paneer finger in the mixture of sauces, roll over crumbs spread on a plate. Gently pass a bamboo stick in it.
5. Heat a flat non stick tawa greased with some oil. Cook the shooters, turning sides till golden on all sides. Serve

NOTE: Extra firm tofu can be used instead of paneer. Zucchini peeled lengthwise with a peeler can also be woven on sticks the same way. Weave 3-4 peels together.

Vermicelli Discs

Serves 4

75 gm (¾ cup) roasted vermicelli (*sewaiyan*)
¼ cup corn, boiled or frozen
½ cup grated carrot
3 tbsp flour (*maida*)
1 tbsp butter
¾-1 cup milk
¼ tsp onion seeds (*kalaunji*)
½ tsp salt, ¼ tsp pepper
½ medium onion - chopped finely
1 tsp green chilli - chopped
1 cheese cube - grated
2-3 drop of lemon juice
2-3 tbsp chopped coriander

1. Boil sewaiyan in 3 cups water with ½ tsp salt for about 3-4 minutes or till soft. Drain and keep aside.
2. Heat butter in a pan, add onion seeds and wait for ½ minute. Add green chilli and onion. Saute till onion turns golden, add flour and stir on low heat for about 2-3 minutes till it smells roasted. Remove from fire.
3. Add milk and stir quickly to avoid lumps. Return to fire. Add carrots. Cook till it starts to turn thick. Reduce heat. Add salt, pepper and cheese and stir. Add corn, coriander leaves, boiled sewaiyan and lemon juice, mix well for 1-2 minutes. Remove from fire and let it cool down.
4. With greased hands, make a tikki like shape and pan fry till golden from both sides on low heat.

Full Meal Snacks

Oriental Sandwich

Makes 6

3-4 big dinner rolls or hot dog buns

butter or mayonnaise to spread, optional

½ red bell pepper - cut into thin juliennes, 1 onion - thinly shredded

7-8 baby corns - each cut lengthwise into 6 very thin, long pieces

3" piece of zucchini or carrot

3 mushrooms - thinly sliced

8-10 fresh whole basil leaves

DRESSING

1 tsp honey

1 tsp lemon juice

2 tsp soya sauce

3 tbsp tomato ketchup

2 tbsp olive oil, 1 tsp cornflour

2 large flakes garlic - grated

¼ tsp pepper, ½ tsp chilli flakes, ½ tsp salt

OTHER INGREDIENTS

curly green lettuce leaves

1. Mix all ingredients of the dressing in a medium bowl.
2. Using a peeler, take out paper thin strips of zucchini or carrot piece. Add these and other vegetables to the dressing and toss to mix well.
3. In a non stick pan, spread out the vegetables and cook for 2-3 minutes without stirring much. Pour the remaining dressing if any on the vegetables. Remove from pan after sauteing veggies for 2-3 minutes. Let it cool to room temperature. Check salt and add a pinch if required.
4. Slit the bun. Lightly butter inside. Open the bun and place the lettuce leaf. Carefully place the filling and close. Grill or serve as it is.

Paneer Shawarma

Serves 4

200 gms paneer - cut into 2" long fingers

1 tomato - deseeded and cut into thin strips, 1 small onion - sliced

3 pita breads - cut into two pieces horizontally to get 2 thin rounds

¼ cup thick yogurt (*dahi*)

½ tsp ginger-garlic paste

some mayonnaise or greek dip, see page 99

MARINADE

1 tsp lemon juice or vinegar

2 tsp Lebanese mixed spices, given on next page

1 tbsp oil

1 tsp salt

1. Marinate paneer with all the ingredients of the marinade for about ½ hour. You can keep it longer if you feel like. In case, you do not have the time to make Lebanese spice powder, use 1 tsp garam masala and crushed seeds of 2-3 green cardamoms instead of 2 tsp spice powder.
2. Heat 1 tbsp oil in a non stick pan, add paneer fingers and stir fry for 3-4 minutes or till slightly golden brown from some sides. Remove from pan.
3. Add onion and tomato slices to the pan and saute for 2 minutes. Reduce heat. Add yogurt and ginger garlic paste. Stir on low heat for a minute. Add paneer. Toss to mix well. Check taste and add a little more lebanese spice if you like. Remove from fire.
4. Warm all the four pieces of pita bread on a hot tawa for 1 minute. Keep one warmed piece on a flat surface. Spread 1 tbsp greek dip, add paneer, tomatoes and onion. Roll forward to make a roll. Serve along with extra dip.

LEBANESE SPICE POWDER

Makes 2 tsp

½ tsp black pepper corns (*saboot kali mirch*)

4-5 cloves (*laung*)

¼ tsp nutmeg (*jaiphal*) - grated

¼ tsp fenugreek seeds (*methi daana*)

¼ tsp ginger (*sonth*) powder

½ tsp green cardamom seeds (*chhoti illaichi ke daane*)

½ tsp fennel (*saunf*)

1 star anise (*phool chakri*)

1" stick cinnamon (*dalchini*)

1. Grind all the ingredients in a small mixer to a powder or crush with a pestle and mortar to a powder. Store in a jar with a tight fitting lid and use as required. It lasts upto six months easily.

Multigrain Desi Wraps

Makes 6

WRAPS

½ cup semolina *(sooji)*, ½ cup gram flour (*besan)*, ½ cup oats

½ cup barely flour (*jaun ka atta*)

2 tbsp green coriander

¾ tsp garam masala, ¼ tsp dry mango powder (*amchoor*)

1 tsp roasted cumin (*jeera*) powder, 1 tsp black salt, ¼ tsp salt

2¼ cups water, approx.

FILLING

1 tbsp oil, 1 tsp panch phoran (a spice blend of 5 spices)

1 onion - sliced, 1 tsp chopped ginger, ¾ tsp salt, ¼ tsp pepper

50 gm paneer or 1 boiled potato - cut into fingers

½ cup boiled/frozen corn or peas, a pinch of sugar, 1 tsp lemon juice

1 tbsp each of coriander and mint, 1 tomato - chopped

1. Mix all ingredients of the wraps. Add enough water gradually to make a pouring pancake batter of coating consistency. Keep aside for 5-10 minutes. Whisk the batter for a minute till smooth.
2. For the filling, heat 1 tbsp oil. Add panch phoran. Wait for a minute. Add onions and chopped ginger. Saute onion till soft. Add boiled potato/paneer and bhuno for a minute.
3. Add corn/peas, salt and pepper. Stir.
4. Add mint and coriander. Stir for a minute. Add tomato. Add a pinch of sugar. Mix. Keep filling aside.
5. To make a pancake, grease a non stick tawa and heat on fire. Remove pan from fire. Pour one kadchhi of batter and spread lightly to a roti size. Return to low heat. Drizzle 1 tsp oil from the sides immediately. Cook for 2-3 minutes till edges turn golden. Turn side and cook the other side on high heat.
6. Put some filling in the centre and roll up to make a wrap. Serve.

Peri Peri Pockets

Makes 8

2 pizza base (medium size)

1 tsp onion seeds (kalaunji)

1 bunch lettuce leaves - dipped in cold water

mayonnaise/cheese spread

CREAMED ONIONS

1 onion - cut into thin slices

1 tbsp chopped basil/coriander

½ tsp lemon juice, ¼ tsp pepper, ¼ tsp salt

VEGETABLES

100 gm babycorns - cut into thin round slices (1 cup)

100 gm mushrooms - cut into 4 and then into slices

1 large red capsicum or yellow capsicum - chopped

1 tbsp butter, 1 tbsp oil

1 tsp chopped garlic, 1 green chilli - chopped

1 tsp chilli garlic spread

3 tbsp ready made tomato puree

½ tsp salt, ½ tsp oregano, pinch of red chilli flakes

2 tbsp mayonnaise/cream

2 tbsp mozarella cheese, optional

GARNISH

olives, lettuce and tooth picks

1. Cut pizza base into 4 pieces. Put under a preheated grill for 2-3 minutes till golden. Let it cool for 2 minutes.
2. Slit each piece carefully. Make a nice pocket using the back of a spoon.
3. Sprinkle lettuce with lemon juice, mayonnaise and a pinch salt. Mix.
4. Heat oil and butter in a big non stick pan. Add garlic and green chillies. When garlic turns fragrant, add onions and stir till golden brown. Add baby corns and saute for 2 minutes. Add mushrooms and saute for 2 minutes.
5. Add red/yellow capsicum, garlic-chilli spread and tomato puree. Mix well and cook for 2-3 minutes. Add salt, oregano and red chilli flakes. Stir for 2 mix. Add mayonnaise or cream. Mix and remove from heat. Add cheese if you like.
6. Mix sliced onions in a bowl with all ingredients to make creamed onions.
7. Open a piece of grilled pocket. Spread mayonnaise or cheese spread inside.
8. Place a lettuce leaf inside. Holding the ungrilled side up, fill a layer of onions inside the pocket. Then put 1 heaped tbsp of vegetables.
9. Preheat the grill of the oven. Place pockets on the grill rack with white side up. Brush with mayonnaise/butter. Sprinkle some onion seeds.
10. To serve grill in the oven for 2-3 minutes or till golden.
11. Garnish with olives on a tooth pick.

Misal Pav

A different kind of pav bhaji made from sprouted beans. Very popular in Mumbai.

Serves 2

1 cup matki/moth bean sprouts

1 potato - peeled and chopped

1 small tomato - chopped

1 tbsp oil

½ onion - chopped, 1 tsp garlic paste

½ tsp turmeric powder (*haldi*)

1 tsp goda masala, use pao bhaji masala if unavailable

1 tsp red chilli powder

1 tsp tamarind pulp

1 tsp jaggery

¾ tsp salt, or to taste

1 tbsp freshly grated coconut

1 tbsp chopped coriander, pav to serve

GARNISH

½ cup sev

½ onion - very finely chopped, 1 tbsp chopped coriander

1. Pressure cook sprouts, potato, tomato with ½ cup water to allow one whistle. Remove from heat. Let the pressure drop by itself.
2. Heat oil. Add onions and garlic paste.
3. Let the onions soften a little. Add turmeric powder, chilli powder and goda masala.
4. Add boiled sprout-potato mixture and 1½ cups water.
5. Add salt, tamarind pulp, jaggery, coconut and coriander. Let it simmer for 5-7 minutes. Leave a little gravy.
6. Garnish with fine sev, chopped onion and coriander. Serve with pav and a lemon wedge.

Couscous Flautas

Makes 10 pieces

½ cup plain flour (*maida*)

¾ cup milk, approx.

¼ tsp salt, ¼ tsp pepper, a pinch of baking powder

FILLING

¼ cup couscous - soaked in ½ cup hot water for 30 minutes

¼ cup very finely chopped green capsicum

¼ cup very finely chopped red capsicum

2 tbsp very finely chopped coriander/parsley

4-5 slices jalapenos - finely chopped

1½ tbsp cheese spread

DRESSING

1 tbsp lemon juice,

2 tbsp extra virgin olive oil

½ tsp salt, ¼ tsp pepper, to taste

¼ tsp crushed cinnamon

¼ tsp roasted cumin (*bhuna jeera*) powder

a pinch of sugar

1. Sift flour, baking powder and salt. Add pepper. Add milk and whisk well to get a smooth pouring consistency. Add a little water if the batter appears thick. Keep aside for 10 minutes.
2. Heat a non-stick tawa (not too hot). Put 1 tsp oil on it. Sprinkle a pinch of salt on the pan. Spread the oil and salt with a paper napkin. Reduce heat and pour a small laddle of batter to make pancakes of 5-6" diameter and cook till both sides light golden. Do not make them crisp and thick. Keep them thin and soft.
3. For the filling, mix all ingredients of the dressing in a medium bowl. Add capsicums (green and red) and mix well. Add couscous, coriander and jalapenos and mix well. Check seasonings.

4. To make flautas, spread 1 tsp of cheese spread on each pancake, specially on the edges. Spread some filling on the pancake and roll up tightly. If needed, use a little cheese spread for sticking the ends. Keep them in a microproof platter with the joint side down. Cover with a wrap till serving time.
5. To serve, cut into into bite sized pieces. Microwave for a minute or grill for 5-7 minutes if you like.

Crispy Quesadillas

makes 16 pieces

4 flour tortillas or very thin flour chappatis

FILLING

½ cup yogurt - hang for 30 minutes (4 tbsp)

½ cup grated paneer

¼ tsp salt and ½ tsp paprika, or to taste

10 slices of jalapenos - chopped finely

1 green chilli - deseeded and very finely chopped

¼ cup cheddar cheese grated and ¼ cup grated mozarella cheese (mix)

1 cup finely chopped green capsicum or zucchini

6-8 mushrooms - wash, slice thinly and microwave for 1 minute

½ small onion - cut into rings

6 tbsp ready made salsa

¼ tsp salt, ¼ tsp pepper

1. For the filling, mix paneer and 4 tbsp hung yogurt. Add salt and paprika to taste. Add very finely chopped jalapenos and deseeded green chilli. Keep aside.
2. Mix raw zucchini/capsicum, onions and blanched mushrooms with salsa, salt and pepper. Check taste.
3. To assemble the quesadillas, place one tortillas on a clean plate. Spread with half of paneer-yogurt spread. Place half of zucchini and mushroom mixed with salsa. Sprinkle half of the grated cheese on it, especially at the edges. Cover with the second tortilla and press well to close the edges. Brush with olive oil.
4. To serve, put on a greased non stick baking tray with oil side down. Brush with oil on the top. Place in the oven at 240°C for about 10-12 minutes till crisp and brown patches appear. Cut into 8 wedges with a pizza cutter and serve.

Stir Fried Salad Wrap

Serves 3-4

3-4 tortillas

3 tbsp olive oil

2 thin long brinjals- cut into slices without peeling

1 small zucchini - cut into slices without peeling (1 cup)

8-10 flakes garlic - sliced

1 large onion - cut into 8 pieces and separated

1 green capsicum - cut into 1" pieces

1 cup cabbage - cut into 1" pieces

8-10 black olives - sliced

1 tbsp vinegar

1 tsp oregano, ¾ tsp pepper

¾ tsp salt

1. Heat 1 tbsp olive oil in a non-stick pan and add the brinjals. Stir fry for 3-4 minutes till brown patches appear. Lower heat, cover & cook for 1 minute till the brinjal pieces are cooked but firm. Remove from pan to a bowl.
2. Heat 1 tbsp oil again in the pan. Add garlic, stir and add onion, zucchini, capsicum and cabbage. Cook for 2 minutes, without stirring much. Remove to the same bowl with brinjals. Add chopped olives to the stir fried vegetables.
3. In a cup, mix vinegar, salt, pepper and oregano. Pour over the stir fried salad and mix well. Keep aside.
4. Place one tortilla on a plate. Put 3 tbsp of the stir-fried veggie mixture in the centre. Fold over once and then holding on, turn the left and right side to enclose the filling. Roll to get a parcel. Repeat with all the tortillas.
5. Heat 1 tbsp oil in a pan and warm the rolls by putting the joint side down in oil first. Turn carefully with a flat spoon when light golden at the bottom. Pan fry the other side for a minute. Cut into 2 pieces. Serve with ketchup.

Toast Supremo

Serves 4

4 brown bread slices - toasted

any sandwich spread or mayonnaise, 1 tbsp butter

2 boiled potatoes - cut into thick round slices, 100 gm paneer - cut into ¼" thick, flat pieces

2-3 green lettuce leaves - dip in chilled water and pat dried on a clean towel, optional

2 small tomatoes - cut into slices

salt, pepper, oregano and red chilli flakes to taste

1 tsp tomato ketchup or mustard sauce

a few fresh basil or coriander leaves, 1 cube cheddar cheese, optional

1. Heat 1 tbsp butter on a non stick tawa or pan. Put potato slices on it. Turn when the under side is light brown. Sprinkle a pinch of salt and pepper. Shift to the sides. Add the paneer slices and saute for 1-2 minutes on medium flame. Add a pinch of salt, pepper, oregano and red chilli flakes. Add ketchup or mustard and mix well. Remove from pan. Put tomatoes also on the hot pan. Remove pan from fire immediately. Sprinkle some salt and pepper on the tomatoes.
2. To serve, make a toast in a toaster while the veggies are being done on the pan. Spread sandwich spread or mayonnaise.
3. Arrange a green salad leaf on the spread. Cover with potato slices.
4. Arrange the tomato slices on the potato slices. Top tomatoes with paneer pieces and then with fresh basil or coriander leaves. Serve immediately or grate cheese finely on it and grill in a hot oven for 2-3 minutes if you like.

Dips for Snacks

Spicy Mustard Dip

SERVES 4-6

3 tbsp mustard sauce, preferably whole grain

1-2 tbsp thick cream

½ tsp red chilli-garlic spread or red chilli flakes

2 tbsp olive oil, or any oil

a few drops honey, a pinch of salt

1. Mix mustard with a little cream, red chilli paste and few drops honey. Add enough olive oil or any cooking oil to thin down the dip. Add salt to taste. This goes very well with continental snacks.

Salsa

Gives 1 cup

6 tomatoes - roasted & peeled (puree 4 and finely chop 2 tomatoes)

2 tbsp oil, ½ onion - chopped finely, ½ tsp chopped garlic

2 green chillies - chopped

2 tbsp roughly torn basil leaves / finely chopped coriander

¼ tsp pepper, ½ tsp salt, ½ tsp sugar

1 tbsp tomato ketchup, 1 tsp vinegar

1. To roast tomatoes, pierce a tomato with a fork. Hold it over the naked gas flame till the skin turns blackish and charred. Roast all the tomatoes like this. Cool and peel. Do not wash after peeling. Chop 2 tomatoes and puree the other 4 in a mixer.
2. Heat 2 tbsp oil, add chopped onion, garlic and green chillies. Cook till onion turns soft. Add all the other ingredients and cook for 2-3 minutes. Remove from fire.

Cheese Dip

Dips can be served with rolls, potato wafers, carrot celery or cucumber sticks or any other starter.

Makes 1 small bowl

1½ cups yogurt - hang in a muslin cloth for 2-3 hours

2 tbsp cheese spread, 100 gms fresh cream

1 medium onion - chopped very fine

1 medium capsicum - deseeded & chopped fine

juice of 1 lemon

salt and white pepper to taste

1. Beat the curd and cheese spread with a baloon whisk till smooth.
2. Mix cream gently.
3. Add all other ingredients and mix lightly. Chill. Serve in a small bowl with starters.

Greek Potato Garlic Dip

Makes 1 *cup*

2 boiled potatoes (medium sized)

4 flakes garlic - crushed or minced (1 tsp), 1 tsp salt, or to taste

¼ cup almonds (*badaam*), vb4 tbsp extra virgin olive oil

4 tbsp water, 2 tbsp lemon juice, 1½ tbsp vinegar, freshly ground pepper

1. Soak almonds in hot water for 15 minutes. Drain. Remove skin from almonds.
2. Combine the garlic, salt, almonds, and oil in a food processor. Blend into a paste.
3. Add potatoes, water, lemon juice & vinegar to the garlic-almond paste. Blend again. Season with pepper. Check seasoning. Remove to a serving bowl. Serve cold or at room temperature with chips, bread sticks or kebabs.

Guacamole

A Mexican dip, served with corn chips.

Makes 1½ *cups*

1 blackish, ripe avocado, 1 small onion - finely chopped

2 green chillies - finely chopped

1 tomato - deseeded and finely chopped

2 tsp finely chopped garlic

½ cup finely chopped coriander

1¼ tsp salt, or to taste, 3-4 tbsp lemon juice

1. Cut an avocado in half. Remove the stone. Scoop out pulp from the avocado with a spoon. Mash pulp with a fork. Add al other ingredients. Mash some more with the fork. Serve chilled or at room temperature. Cover with a plastic wrap/cling film as guacamole tends to turn brown on keeping.

Smoked Red Pepper Dip

1 red bell pepper
1 dry red chilli - soaked in water and microwave for 1 minute
1 flake garlic - finely chopped
½ tsp salt
¼ tsp paprika
1 tsp cheese spread
½ tsp lemon juice
1/3 cup extra virgin olive oil
a pinch of red chilli flakes
a pinch of fresh or dry parsley

1. Roast a washed red bell pepper on a naked flame for about 5 minutes till nicely black all over. Immediately put in a bowl and cover the bowl for 10 minutes for the pepper to sweat and acquire a nice smoky flavour. Peel the black skin. Wash your hands and peel again nicely but do not wash the pepper. Deseed the pepper and chop roughly. Keep aside.
2. In a small spice grinder, put drained and softened dry red chilli cut into bits, garlic, salt and paprika. Grind to a rough paste.
3. To the grinder add - chopped roasted pepper and grind again till smooth.
4. Add 1 tsp cheese spread, ½ tsp lemon juice and 1/3 cup olive oil to the pepper in the grinder and grind again for a few seconds.
5. Add red chilli flakes and oregano. Remove to a small micro proof serving bowl. To serve, warm in a microwave for 30 seconds.
6. Serve as a dip with nachos, pizza crackers or with vegetable crudites.

Spices

Asafoetida (Hing)

Black Cumin Seeds (Shah Jeera)

Brown Mustard Seed (Rai)

Cinnamon (dalchini)

Cloves (Laung)

Coriander Seeds (Saboot Dhania)

Cumin Seeds (Jeera)

Cardamom (Chhoti Elaichi)

Carom Seeds (Ajwain)

Fennel Seeds (Saunf)

Mace (Javitri)

Melon Seeds (Magaz)

Nutmeg (Jaiphal)

Nigella, Onion Seeds (Kalaunji)

Poppy Seeds (Khus-Khus)

Sesame Seeds (Til)

International Conversion Guide

These are not exact equivalents; they've been rounded-off to make measuring easier.

WEIGHTS & MEASURES

Metric	Imperial
15 g	½ oz
30 g	1 oz
60 g	2 oz
90 g	3 oz
125 g	4 oz (¼ lb)
155 g	5 oz
185 g	6 oz
220 g	7 oz
250 g	8 oz (½ lb)
280 g	9 oz
315 g	10 oz
345 g	11 oz
375 g	12 oz (¾ lb)
410 g	13 oz
440 g	14 oz
470 g	15 oz
500 g	16 oz (1 lb)
750 g	24 oz (1 ½ lb)
1 kg	30 oz (2 lb)

LIQUID MEASURES

Metric	Imperial
30 ml	1 fluid oz
60 ml	2 fluid oz
100 ml	3 fluid oz
125 ml	4 fluid oz
150 ml	5 fluid oz (¼pint/1 gill)
190 ml	6 fluid oz
250 ml	8 fluid oz
300 ml	10 fluid oz (½ pint)
500 ml	16 fluid oz
600 ml	20 fluid oz (1 pint)
1000 ml	1¾ pints

CUPS & SPOON MEASURES

Metric	Imperial
1 ml	¼ tsp
2 ml	½ tsp
5 ml	1 tsp
15 ml	1 tbsp
60 ml	¼ cup
125 ml	½ cup
250 ml	1 cup

HELPFUL MEASURES

Metric	Imperial
3 mm	1/8 in
6 mm	¼ in
1 cm	½ in
2 cm	¾ in
2.5 cm	1 in
5 cm	2 in
6 cm	2½ in
8 cm	3 in
10 cm	4 in
13 cm	5 in
15 cm	6 in
18 cm	7 in
20 cm	8 in
23 cm	9 in
25 cm	10 in
28 cm	11 in
30 cm	12 in (1 ft)

HOW TO MEASURE

When using the graduated metric measuring cups, it is important to shake the dry ingredients loosely into the required cup. Do not tap the cup on the table, or pack the ingredients into the cup unless otherwise directed. Level top of cup with a knife. When using graduated metric measuring spoons, level top of spoon with a knife. When measuring liquids in the jug, place jug on a flat surface, check for accuracy at eye level.

OVEN TEMPERATURE

These oven temperatures are only a guide. Always check the manufacturer's manual.

	°C (Celsius)	°F (Fahrenheit)	Gas Mark
Very low	120	250	1
Low	150	300	2
Moderately low	160	325	3
Moderate	180	350	4
Moderately high	190	375	5
High	200	400	6
Very high	230	450	7

BEST SELLING COOKBOOKS BY SNAB

SNAB
Excellence in Books

Cookbook of Rajasthan

Cookbook for Festivals of India

101 Recipes for Children

Permanent Weight Loss Cookbook

Italian cooking for the Indian kitchen

Different ways with Paneer

Indian cooking with Olive Oil

Traditional & Innovative MITHAI

PUNJABI Khaana

Mother & Child Cookbook

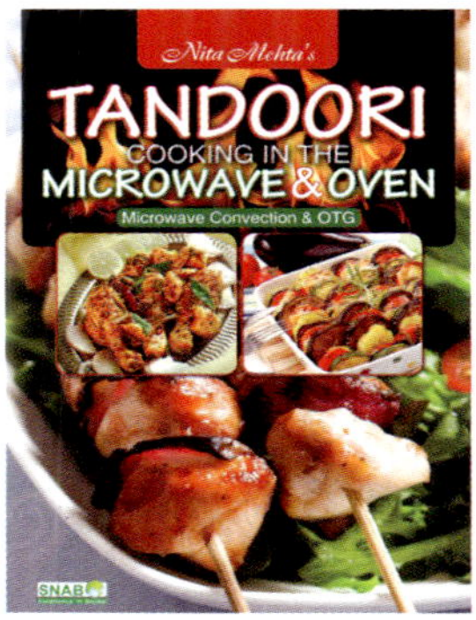

Tandoori cooking in the Microwave & Oven

101 Vegetarian Recipes

Eggless Cakes & Muffins

Microwave Desi Khaana

Fish & Prawns

101 Diet Recipes

BEST SELLING COOKBOOKS BY SNAB Excellence in Books

Cookbook for Controlling Diabetes

Indian Vegetarian Favourites

Tasty & Nutritious Oats Cookbook

Learn to Cook Pizza & Pasta

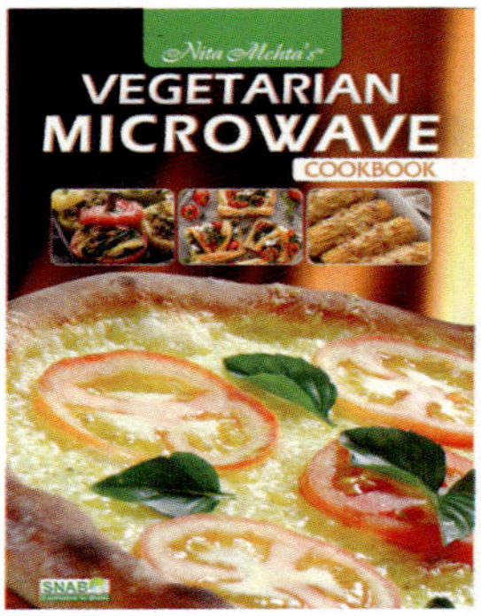

Vegetarian Microwave Cookbook

Mocktails & Starters

Cakes & Cake Decorations

Zero Oil Cooking

Snacks for Children

Leran to Cook Chinese

Great Indian Cooking

Burgers & Sandwiches

ASIAN Cookbook

Bakes & Cakes

LEBANESE cooking for the Indian kitchen

Soups & Salads

BEST SELLERS BY SNAB

Excellence in Books

Biryanis & Pulaos

Baking Recipes

All Time Snacks

Corn & Pasta - Vegetarian

Drinks & Indian Desserts

Tiffin Recipes

Cooking Under 10 Minutes

Taste of Rajasthan - Vegetarian

Vegetarian Curries

Snacks & Desserts

Tikka Seekh & Kebab

Taste of Hyderabad - Vegetarian

Baby Cookbook

Breakfast Recipes

Cook in Minutes

Chatpati Chaat

Cakes & Cookies

Delicious Home made Ice Cream

Green Vegetables

Food for Children

Mocktails & Snacks

Microwave Recipes – Vegetarian

Microwave Cakes & Snacks

Taste of Delhi

Snacks & Chaat

Paneer Recipes

Saatvik Khaana

Party Food